52 THINGS SONS need from their MOMS

angela Thomas

HARVEST HOUSE PUBLISHERS
EUGENE, OREGON

Cover by Left Coast Design, Portland, Oregon

Cover photo © Cultura / Inmagine

52 THINGS SONS NEED FROM THEIR MOMS
Copyright © 2015 Angela Thomas
Published by Harvest House Publishers
Eugene, Oregon 97402
www.harvesthousepublishers.com

Library of Congress Cataloging-in-Publication Data
    Thomas, Angela, 1962-
    52 things sons need from their moms / Angela Thomas.
       pages cm
    ISBN 978-0-7369-5221-7 (pbk.)
    ISBN 978-0-7369-5222-4 (eBook)
    1. Mothers and sons—Religious aspects—Christianity. I. Title. II. Title: Fifty-two things sons need from a mom.
    BV4529.18.T4495 2015
    248.8'431—dc23

                                 2014042009

Printed in the United States of America

       15 16 17 18 19 20 21 22 23 / VP-JH / 10 9 8 7 6 5 4 3 2 1

Contents

A Son Needs His Mom to

Stay Close to Jesus

For God so loved the world, that he gave his only Son, that whoever believes in him should not perish but have eternal life. For God did not send his Son into the world to condemn the world, but in order that the world might be saved through him.

John 3:16-17

Hello, new friend.

Today I wish we were meeting for coffee instead of this awkward first time meeting on a page. For months now, I've tried to imagine what you look like. Where you live. The age and stage of your son. Is he fast asleep on your lap right this minute? This book propped on his blanket or toy? Did your boy just yell, "I love you, Mom," and then run into the backyard to play? Are you grabbing this moment, having lunch in your office while your son is at school or day care? Are you in the car pool line? Sitting on the floor during nap time? Waiting outside the door of his music lesson?

Oh man, I really wish we were having coffee. I'd love to hear all about him.

Words on a page feel like such a clumsy way for me to start because the very thing that could make all the difference is missing. Tone. Countenance. Laughter. A smirk. A wink. A tear. I long for you to know I'm beside you. I'm not writing to you from a soapbox. I'm not typing from some academic, far-removed setting. Girl, I'm on your team! The moms of boys are my people. Shoot, if you lived on my street, we'd have to be friends.

Maybe this will help. I've been trying to imagine where you are, so here's an honest picture of me, this very minute.

I work at home, so here I am. In my house, there's an "office" for me, but it's been torn up for months. Every office kind of thing I own is piled into boxes all over. A guy is in there today building bookshelves, so I'm on the other side of the house in my bedroom. I have my laptop and a couple of books beside me; my feet are dangling over the side of the bed. For the past month I've been wearing the same version of a writing uniform. Gym shorts, a T-shirt, and flip-flops. No makeup, of course. My kids are teenagers and there's no school today, so my door keeps going open, close, open, close, open, close. Every time it opens, I forget what I'm writing because we start talking about nothing. Surely anyone could write faster than a mom with chatty teenagers, holed up in her bedroom while the sound of a nail gun pops the air.

I may be a few years ahead of you, but I hope you can still hear my heart. I'm on your team. I am for you. These words about raising sons are written for you as encouragement, without judgment. Probably a lot like you, I arrived at this gigantic task completely unqualified, and I've been in over my head ever since. As we begin these pages of encouragement together, I want to start with the most important things.

If I have done anything right as a mom, it is because of Jesus Christ. And if the things I've done wrong don't completely ruin my sons forever, it is, again, only because of Jesus.

I have no idea about your faith tradition, so there is no way to know what the name of Jesus means to you. Here is what Jesus means to me:

I grew up around people who talked about Jesus and attended a church where people worshipped Him. Until I was older, most of what I knew about Him I had learned from my parents and my church.

Then a college education taught me to ask questions and eventually I began to ask questions about my faith. *What about Jesus? Was He really who He said? Is He the Son of God? Did He die on a cross and then, three days later, walk from His tomb, alive?*

So I searched and studied, read and researched, and asked all the questions until my soul was satisfied. Over and over, the answer was *yes*, Jesus truly is the Son of God. The Old Testament promised a Messiah and Jesus is the fulfillment of that promise. Jesus lived on this earth and died on a cross. Three days later, He was raised to life. Over five hundred people saw the resurrected Jesus. The Bible is the record of God's love and contains His wisdom for our lives.

If Jesus Christ is the Son of God, the only logical decision I could make was to follow Him. He had to become the center of my life. Today my faith is filled with emotion, but deciding to follow Jesus wasn't an emotional decision for me. Becoming a Christ follower was the logical result of an honest search.

I tell you my journey because I want you to understand the weight of my words. The first lesson in this book is not intended to be spiritual or emotional or holier-than-thou-sounding. I've begun with this first thing because it's the most important thing I have to offer. Your son needs you to trust Christ and stay close to Him.

Trusting Christ is not about keeping a tradition. Or sitting in a church. Or doing good things with church people. If you don't know Jesus, it would be my honor to introduce you. He is the Lord of all, but more than that, the Bible says He loves you with an everlasting kind of love and He designed you to be in relationship with Him. The Bible says anyone who believes Jesus is Lord can run to Him.

He is the only One able to forgive you and make you clean.

His words are the only words with the power to change your life.

His way is the only way to find rest for your weary soul.

He is the One who wants to redeem your brokenness and heal your wounds.

He is faithful, the Protector of all you entrust to His care.

Maybe you've heard someone say, "I couldn't have made it without Jesus." That's exactly how I feel. There is no way to become the mom my son needs apart from an alive and growing relationship with Jesus Christ.

The most important thing you will ever do is become a follower of Jesus Christ. And you can make that decision wherever you are. The God who loves you is not far off; He's right there with you now. Becoming a follower is not about returning to an empty tradition. Becoming a follower means your whole life gets reorganized around Christ at the center.

My new mom friend, I pray you'll trust Jesus and stay close to Him.

Truth is, you really don't need the rest of my words. I hope they mean something to you and I hope you'll be inspired. But if you're looking for the power to become a great mom to your son or the power to change midstream or the power to endure the trial you face, I cannot give you that.

Jesus is the One you need.

2

A Son Needs His Mom to

Be Filled with the Powerful, Everyday Grace of God

But he gives more grace.

James 4:6

A*good mom does all the right things.*

I hope some of you just threw this book across the coffee shop, declaring to no one in particular, "I quit." Maybe you just whipped out your laptop and began typing a response for your next blog post. But maybe those words made you sit up straight. The tingle of challenge raced through your veins and you whispered to yourself, *I've got this.* At first glance, it kind of sounds noble, don't you think? *Good moms do all the right things.*

That nice little platitude sounds true enough until reality wakes you from your dream. The bright room tells you it's happened again—the whole entire family overslept. You rush the kids into their mismatched clothes and hurry them out to the bus. They clutch stale doughnuts and Gatorades instead of the healthy breakfast you intended. You kiss their sleepy heads, give the bus driver an *I'm-sorry* wave, and then stand for a moment to let your pounding heart slow. It's a quick shuffle back into the kitchen and straight to the coffeepot, where you declare to the dog, *If good moms do all the right things, I'm disqualified.*

There is a passage in the Bible that says, "For it is by grace you have been saved, through faith—and this is not from yourselves, it is the gift of God—not by works, so that no one can boast" (Ephesians 2:8-9). When I became a follower of Jesus, I understood God's gift of salvation came to me by grace. I did not deserve His gift, nor was there anything I could have done to be found deserving. God's grace is a gift that cannot be earned. The grace given to us at salvation is a huge, beautiful theological truth. But that grace is only the beginning. God continues to give grace to His followers and that grace is the means by which we live and walk in real godliness.

A lot of people can spend a lifetime trying to earn their way. Mistaken, they believe if they just do the right thing, then life with all its challenges will turn out fine. *If my grades are good enough. If I keep the rules perfectly. If I don't cause a stir and keep on the straight and narrow and never have anything to do with those people. If I give my time and my money and my energy. If I do and do and do and do. And if I make them happy. Then maybe, just maybe, life will go well for me.*

Lord, have mercy. That is the woman I have been. And sadly, that woman first became my kids' mom.

It hurts to remember.

When a mom mistakenly believes *doing everything right* → *good kids with a good life*, the Bible might call her a Pharisee. Pharisees believed keeping the rules made you a better person. Trying so hard is the kind of thing you don't notice at first, like dark clouds slipping onto the horizon. Without a miraculous change, the doing-everything-right hurricane in your heart means a disastrous storm is headed your way.

It's the easiest thing in the world to transfer all of our unrealistic expectations onto our children.

Maybe they'll do right for all the things we didn't do right.

Or maybe they'll take all our right things and make them even better.

And surely there will be some great cosmic return with blessings to reward all our goodness.

I think I bought into the Supermom fantasy with good intentions. Years went by and the storm clouds grew darker and the harder I worked at "being," the more graceless my life became. Worst of all, there were little eyes watching every move.

A Bible scholar who knew plenty about grace for salvation, I was also a proud woman missing the everyday grace of God for my soul. Finding God's everyday grace for my life was the grace that set me free. The grace my children desperately needed. And the grace that miraculously sent the hurricane I was becoming out to sea.

The women in my life at that time were pivotal in showing me what grace for this life looks like and sounds like and feels like. I love what Joanna Weaver wrote: "I didn't know I was dry until I got around people who were wet."* I had lived so very dry without grace and truly didn't know another way. Maybe today, you don't know another way either. I pray this will be the day God's grace begins to fall like rain for your dry soul.

> Out of his fullness we have all received grace in place of grace already given (John 1:16).

> Let us then approach God's throne of grace with confidence, so that we may receive mercy and find grace to help us in our time of need (Hebrews 4:16).

> But grow in the grace and knowledge of our Lord and Savior Jesus Christ (2 Peter 3:18).

Grace makes hard women soft. Grace makes angry women glad. Grace forgives the unforgiven. Grace buries the grudge. Grace loves the unlovely and sees potential where the world sees none. Grace looks past the flaws again and again and again. Grace doesn't give up on anybody for any reason. Grace always hopes, always dreams, always believes, always tries.

When a mom grabs hold of the grace of God, then by that power she is set free. She is free to forgive herself and her family. She is free to see what really matters in life and then run after it. She is free to laugh with her children and to embrace the quirks of her husband. She is free to endure hardship and suffering, to rejoice in success, and search for her passion.

Is God speaking to you today? Don't you want to be free? Jesus says all who ask can be free indeed.

Your son needs a mom who is filled with the lavish, everyday grace of God. Second to following Jesus, this is the most powerful, life-giving,

---

* Joanna Weaver, *Having a Mary Heart in a Martha World* (Colorado Springs, CO: WaterBrook Publishers, 2000), 145.

peace-bestowing gift you will bring into his life. My favorite seminary professor, Dr. Howard Hendricks, said more times than I can recount, "You cannot impart what you do not possess." The truth of those words speaks deeply to me as a mom. We cannot give our sons a grace we do not have.

To be filled with grace is to receive God's full acceptance of you, just as you are. He has always known your limitations and your strengths, but the God who knows you truly loves you still. Even if you never get any better at anything in this life, the good news is you never had anything to prove anyway. You are His. Would you let the grace of God fill your heart and make you free?

To be filled with grace is to possess the very thing God wants you to give to your son. When you live from grace, your son may perform well or fail, but neither has the power to change his mom's love. Filled with God's grace means the condition of his soul matters more than schedules and rules and appearances. By grace, God's love becomes your measure so your son's grades and rankings cannot assign his worth. Your faith is in God and your eyes are on Him, so your son is off the hook. He doesn't have to grow up and become your savior. When you live in grace, your son watches you lay the cares of this world on the altar of God. You make decisions for your son with eternity in view, not knee-jerk reactions made from worry or fear.

How about a revised, grace-filled definition? A good mom is doing the best she can from the fullness of God's grace.

May it be said of you and of me, *She was full of grace, and that made all the difference.*

3

A Son Needs His Mom to

Build a Legacy of Grace

For from his fullness we have all received, grace upon grace.

John 1:16

Afew years ago, our family had several talks about inviting an international student to come live with us. I was having one of those conversations with the boys when I said, "Guys, I just feel like that student, whoever he is, needs to be forewarned."

"Mom, what are you talking about, *forewarned*?" one asked.

"Well, you know, someone should tell him what kind of people we are. He may not want to live with a family like us. Seems like he should know in advance that we have rules," I explained.

Eighteen and sixteen years old at the time, both boys looked at me across the kitchen counter like I had finally lost my mind. Then, in stereo and complete honesty, they asked, "What rules?"

I stood there for just a second and smiled. Then I almost cried with joy. It was one of my best mom moments ever. My nearly grown boys, with their big eyes and blank faces, did not know we had rules. So I began to list a few. "We have rules. Like, no one can sneak out of the house by cover of night and run down to the corner to buy drugs. You cannot lie. You cannot stay out later than we agreed." My list was just getting on a roll when they interrupted.

"Oh, yeah. Okay, yeah." Now the boys understood. "You should probably make sure he knows that stuff in advance."

Praise God, those two sons of mine laughed out loud when I told them our family has rules. *Oh, thank You, Jesus. It's only by Your grace.*

If the grace of the Lord God Almighty had not taken hold of me in my early mom years, I'm afraid my teenage sons would have been marking the days until they were free of the jail I had built. The riches of God's grace truly changed my nature. Only grace can make a home with strong rules feel like the most peaceful, easy place on earth. I'm so grateful God's grace set this rule-keeping, uptight, do-it-all-right mom free. Do you know what it looks like where grace lives?

When grace breaks the supermom out of jail then your home becomes the place where grace lives. All the neighborhood kids want to hang out at the house where grace lives. There is more dirt to be swept, there are more snacks to be made, and the grass doesn't grow outside the back door or underneath the swing. But kids show up and hang out and get loved where grace lives.

The dust may be a little thicker on top of the TV and the closets a bit cluttered, but hearts have been tended where grace lives. Family management has become the tool instead of the goal. Schedules matter, but souls matter more.

There is always enough for one more where grace lives. One more for dinner. One more to sleep over. One more hug. One more kiss.

The lights are on late where grace lives. Grace stays up to listen, hug in the dark, and wipe away tears of disappointment and pain.

You can see people dancing where grace lives, because moms hang up the phone, turn up the music, and dance over the victories of their children. Then sometimes, children just watch from behind their cereal and "catch" the grace of a silly mom.

You can hear things like, "Please forgive me, I was wrong. I'm disappointed, but I love you. You are my treasure. You are my blessing. Let me pray for you."

Rules at the house where grace lives are wise boundaries whose purpose is protection. Grace knows how to build strong bars of rules into thick walls of love. And when rules are wrapped in love, they are almost unseen.

The eyes of the children where grace lives shine with joy and anticipation. They have not been wounded by impossible expectations. They have not been distanced by rejection. They are embraced and accepted and loved.

The moms at the house where grace lives are just regular, everyday moms, but God lives inside them. By His power, they are becoming holy and righteous and good. They stumble but recover quickly. They make mistakes but say, "I'm sorry." They get blown by the same winds of adversity, but their hearts remain tender toward God.

The mom at the home where grace lives knows the difference God's grace brings. She realizes His grace through her is one of the most powerful gifts she has to give. She knows being a mom requires more grace than she has, so she stays close to Jesus for His supply.

Raising a son these days requires a mom to possess a balance of strength and grace. I have honestly never felt like I was enough of either…and the balance part, well, I may never get that down. But the sweet awareness of my great lack keeps me doing one thing every single day. I run to Jesus. And then I run to Jesus. And I run to Jesus.

Here's what I know for sure. Jesus will supply all the grace you need.

One of the most surprising realizations about grace in my life was learning that grace is the dominant power. Or as my little guys used to ask, "Mom, if you could have one superpower, which one would it be?" Now I know the answer. Leaping tall buildings and x-ray vision are nothing compared to grace. The fullness of grace is stronger than angry emotions. It is stronger than lost perspective and foolish decisions. It's more powerful than pouting little boys and rebellious teenage boys. When you are filled with grace, God can give a greater wisdom and discernment than you have ever known. More authority and patience and peace than I ever experienced has come with the powerful gift of God's grace.

From the fullness of grace, God changed the focus of my parenting so that the condition of my son's heart became my primary concern. His heart is at the center of my prayers for him and it's my first consideration in every situation or decision I make for him.

Is his heart good? Are his motives humble or self-centered? What will this decision do in his heart? How will my words affect his heart?

Then I ask God, by His grace, to help me see clearly. That my discernment would be honest, not distorted by my feelings.. That I would not be a mom who wears blinders when I look at him. Nor would I be the mom who bombards her son with scathing analytics. As much as I am able, I want to see him like God does. Considering my son's heart has become my constant guide, especially through these teenage years. If I consider his heart first...

- The more important heart issue is addressed and not just the action.

- I am able to see pain I might have missed when I only reacted to a situation.

- My discipline tethered to grace keeps strong consequences from becoming undeserved punishment.

- His virtues are not hidden behind his mistakes and unnoticed.

- Laughter comes more easily for me when there is a good heart and an honest mistake.

Grace changed everything for me. My focus. My tone. My countenance. My joy. So truly, if I could give my son one superpower, the superpower of God's grace would be the one.

May the grace of God become your superpower. And may you build a legacy of grace for your son.

4

A Son Needs His Mom to
Pray

Be constant in prayer.

Romans 12:12

Thomas is five years old and maybe the most adorable child you ever laid eyes on. His mom is my dear friend, neighbor, and wonderful blogger, Amy Heywood.* When Thomas began kindergarten this year, Amy sent me a new version of the same picture every day his first week. After school Amy would get Thomas first and then drive around the building where they'd wait for his sisters. Every afternoon around car pool time, I received a new picture of Thomas buckled into his car seat. Fast asleep. Kindergarten was obviously exhausting.

Then a few days ago, Amy sent this text: "Kids and I were praying on the way to school and girls and I were praying about everyday, smallerish stuff, help through the day basic kind of stuff, and when it got to Thomas he said, 'God, please give me power to conquer kingdoms. Amen.' Apparently, Thomas's opinion is go big or go home. A man after God's own heart…"

Oh my goodness. Tucked inside the heart of the cutest kindergarten boy ever is the heart of the man he is becoming. I join Thomas and pray Hebrews 11:32-34 over him:

> *Father, I pray for our Thomas. May he become a man like the faithful who came before us. May he become like those of whom it is written:*

---

* You can find Amy's blog at www.playingsublimely.com.

"And what more shall I say? I do not have time to tell about Gideon, Barak, Samson and Jephthah, about David and Samuel and the prophets, who through faith conquered kingdoms, administered justice, and gained what was promised; who shut the mouths of lions, quenched the fury of the flames, and escaped the edge of the sword; whose weakness was turned to strength; and who became powerful in battle and routed foreign armies."

In Jesus's name, amen.

Your son needs a mom who will pray for the man he is becoming. A mom who asks others to pray for him. A mom who prays the powerful truth of Scripture over him and for him.

A sweet friend just gave me a journal and on every page a Bible verse was printed at the bottom with my name inserted into the verse. Can I tell you how much a verse comes alive when you read your own name within its words? In exactly the same way, we can pray the Scriptures for our sons. I hope the verses below help you begin praying Scripture for your son. But don't let this list be all there is. Sit with your Bible and read with your heart and pray those Scriptures over his life. Go ahead and insert your son's name into the blanks.

And they said, "_____, believe in the Lord Jesus, and you will be saved, you and your household" (Acts 16:31).

_____, grow in the grace and knowledge of our Lord and Savior Jesus Christ. To him be glory both now and forever! Amen (2 Peter 3:18).

Be strong and courageous, _____. Do not be afraid or terrified because of them, for the LORD your God goes with you; he will never leave you nor forsake you (Deuteronomy 31:6).

Create in _____ a pure heart, O God, and renew a steadfast spirit within him (Psalm 51:10).

Be merciful, _____, just as your Father is merciful (Luke 6:36).

Rejoice always, _____ (1 Thessalonians 5:16).

Don't let anyone look down on _____ because he is young, but let him set an example for the believers in speech, in conduct, in love, in faith and in purity (1 Timothy 4:12).

_____, you can do all this through him who gives you strength (Philippians 4:13).

May the God of hope fill _____ with all joy and peace as he trusts in him, so that _____ may overflow with hope by the power of the Holy Spirit (Romans 15:13).

5

A Son Needs His Mom to

Teach Him About the Great Love of God

Hear, O Israel: The LORD our God, the LORD is one. You shall love the LORD your God with all your heart and with all your soul and with all your might. And these words that I command you today shall be on your heart. You shall teach them diligently to your children, and shall talk of them when you sit in your house, and when you walk by the way, and when you lie down, and when you rise. You shall bind them as a sign on your hand, and they shall be as frontlets between your eyes. You shall write them on the doorposts of your house and on your gates.

Deuteronomy 6:4-9

William had just turned four years old. He was a cute little pumpkin back then, but he was also incredibly sneaky. One afternoon, William and the other children had finished their snacks. With my usual pre-supper instructions, all their grazing had officially been suspended. I told them, "That's it. No more, no sirree, nothing else until dinner. Nada."

"But I'm still hungry," William declared.

Sweet mom smile. Bended knee. Eye to eye with his cuteness. "I'm so glad you're hungry because I am making a great dinner, and you're gonna love it. Hang on, buddy. It won't be long."

I went back to working on dinner, distracted by homework and the baby. A little while later, William was trying to walk extra-quietly through the kitchen with one hand behind his back. I realized he'd been standing in the pantry.

"Hey William, whatcha doing?" I asked.

"Nothin'."

"Honey, come here and look at Mommy."

There was a painful, obedient shuffle over toward me while one hand remained attached to his back. Finally standing closer, his huge brown eyes turned their blank stare upward. His solemn little face was intent and serious. Oreo cookie crumbs fell gently from his lips.

"Whatcha got?"

"Nothin'."

"Are you sure?"

"Yes, ma'am." At four he had already learned the fine art of manners in times of trouble.

"William, do you remember what happens when you tell a lie?"

"Yes, ma'am. Big twuble."

"And what happens when you tell the truth?"

"Mur-cee."

"William, do you want to tell me the truth? I'll wait for you to decide."

There was silence. A long silence. So I just stood there watching his four-year-old brain process the options. You could almost see what was bouncing around in there. *Big twuble. Mur-cee. Big twuble. Murcee. Let me see, which one do I want?* "Big twuble" must have been a strong contender because arriving at the truth took longer than I'd expected.

Eventually, a grimy little hand slowly emerged from behind his back and revealed its contents. Two Oreo cookies.

"Thank you, William. Because you told me the truth, you are not going to lose any privileges. But because you disobeyed Mommy, you will need to stand in the corner for five minutes. I want you to think about what you have done."

"That's mur-cee?" he asked.

"Yes, sweetie. That's mercy."*

At four years old, William already knew how to smuggle contraband and lie about it. The Bible says the innate ability to smuggle and lie, with absolutely no training, comes from our sin nature. We have all come to

---

* Excerpted from *Tender Mercy for a Mother's Soul* by Angela Thomas, a Focus on the Family book published by Tyndale House Publishers, Inc. © 2001, 2006 by Angela Thomas. Used by permission.

earth with the ability to sin. Left to their sin nature, little boys, like William, can become grown men still trying to do the same thing with God. Hiding dark places behind their back, solemn faces with blank stares, acting as if God doesn't know or can't see.

When a grown man has not understood the great love of God, he has missed the goodness of God's compassion, His forgiveness, and His mercy. Fear determines his choices. Shame becomes his burden. The consequences of sin are his wounds.

As moms, we have no greater privilege than teaching our sons about the great love of God. Our parenting is the perfect opportunity to become imitators of God's character. Even imperfect moms can point their sons to our perfect Father. He is the One who loves us enough to put life on hold until we bring what is hidden into the light. The One who demonstrated His love for us by sending His only Son so we can be forgiven. The One who expresses His love as mercy. And grace. And peace. And comfort. And on and on.

The Old Testament book of Deuteronomy instructs parents to use the daily routines of life to teach their children. When you sit in your house. When you walk and talk. When you lie down. When you rise. In the heart of a little boy, the lessons of God's great love have the power to shape his character early.

With my sons, I am trying to err on the side of love. I want to discipline them like a woman who knows about God's love instead of giving the discipline that comes from my frustration. I want to respond to him with the patience God gives to me, instead of barking, "Get to the point," from my hurriedness.

Ever since they were born, I have been intentionally trying to teach my children about the great love of God. But oh, my goodness, more days than I can count, my best intentional effort totally missed it. Even worse were the days I lost my focus, looking at myself instead of the love of God. Those selfish days are the days I caused pain.

Here is the obvious truth: Imperfect moms are many days an inadequate and incomplete representation of God's love. And then here is the crazy, astounding truth about God's love for moms. It's almost more than

I can take in: My flawed attempts to represent God's love are also covered by His grace.

The great love of God astounds me.

When the intent of your heart is to glorify God in your home and to love your children as God has loved you, then time and time again, you will find His grace covers your imperfections.

Hide yourself in Him. And with everyday things, in everyday ways, teach your son that God is love.

6

A Son Needs His Mom to

Remember She Must
Release Him to Manhood

*For a man's ways are before the eyes of the
Lord, and he ponders all his paths.*

Proverbs 5:21

A cute woman patiently waited to speak to me after a conference in Alabama. When we finally had a few moments together she said, "You mentioned you are writing a book for moms about sons."

Excited she remembered something said in passing, I responded, "Yes, yes I am. Do you have sons?"

"I have three wonderful grown sons and they're all married to great women. I also have four grandchildren," she answered. While she spoke I got a better look. She was the kind of woman who didn't look old enough to have high schoolers, much less grown sons. She seemed happy and smart and I immediately enjoyed her countenance. Our conversation was interesting and easy. At some point I told her I have boys and girls and said something like, "Some days it feels easier to raise boys."

Her eyes softened with the kind of wisdom I don't yet have, and then, just like she had planned our entire conversation, she said, "Boys are easy to raise and tough to release." I didn't think I could breathe. Her eyes filled with tears as she continued: "Releasing my sons has been the hardest thing I've had to do in my life. Today they are all good men, married to women I love, and it's still hard." By that time I was about to sob. *Release my sons?* Are you kidding me? I mean, I know they're growing up but what in the world? I don't want to think about it. I can't think about it.

25

She asked, "Have you ever heard the one thing standing between a boy and his manhood is his mom? When you want him to become a great man, a mom has to set herself aside and let him go. I've found the best thing I can do for his manhood at this stage is to pursue a deep relationship with his wife. My love has not changed but I had to willingly pull back."

That night in Alabama, I headed back to my hotel a stunned, teary, crybaby mess. Listening to that brave mom, I was sure she was telling the truth. Releasing my sons into manhood one day might be the toughest thing I'll ever do. Honestly, I can hardly write through my tears right now. I've spent their lifetimes trying to keep them close. She reminded me the time is even shorter now. Soon, it will be time to let go.

Great men don't grow up and organize their life around their mama. I know that. They don't wait to make a decision until they call their mom. Or run home and talk through their day with her. Great men don't keep living with their mom or remain financially dependent on their mom. A great man still loves his mom, but she cannot remain the center of his world.

A mom is called to help build the foundation of her son's heart—a strong foundation that enables him to grow into manhood. From the very beginning, I understood the goal in raising a son was that he becomes a strong, independent, capable man of God. When each one of them was born, I thanked God for the privilege of raising a son. I could not love my daughters any more than I do, but we live in a world desperately in need of great men. So if somehow, some way, my sons become great men in this world, my job as their mom will have been done.

From our son's birth, we must keep the goal in mind. The goal is to raise a godly, mature man who is responsible and ready for manhood. The enormity of that goal seems impossible when we are so well acquainted with our inadequacy. So we fall on our knees every night and beg the Lord to change us and lead us and use us and then, even in spite of us, shape these baby boys into great men.

As you and I keep his manhood in view, the way to great character is made clear. From the time he's a little boy, teach your son…

- The value of the Bible as the Word of God. A great man builds his life on the rock of Jesus Christ.

- The joy of what he already has. Great men know having the next thing never brings true joy.

- Life is more than spending. Don't buy him something every time you go into a store. Great men have learned to prioritize their wants and spend wisely.

- The importance of being responsible. Don't save him every time by running forgotten papers to school or misplaced cleats to practice. It's okay to take a zero in class or do push-ups at practice for forgetting. Great men are responsible and remember.

- It is more honorable to go last. Great men lead with a servant's heart. Jesus said the first shall be last and the last shall be first.

- A zero-tolerance policy for disrespect. He cannot disrespect you or his sister or a stranger or authority. Great men give equal honor across humanity. Women are equal. Different ethnicities are equal. People of different opinions and faiths are still equal. Great men have strong opinions and disagree without disrespectful behavior.

- To never ignore another's need if he is able to help. Great men lift up others every time they can. They understand this world is not one big competition and we're in this thing together. They know the power of Proverbs 3:27: "Do not withhold good from those to whom it is due, when it is in your power to act."

- To turn his eyes away from what is inappropriate to see. Great men honor the beauty of women and do not dishonor that beauty with porn. Great men have a reverence for life and do not dishonor life by viewing the horrific and gruesome.

- It's not all about him. Don't always ask him where he'd like to go or what he'd like to do or what he wants to eat. Great men plan for the happiness of others.

- Healthy choices are better and unhealthy choices are deceitful. Teach him the momentary pleasure of sugar (or whatever) hides the greater harms it does to your body. Great men understand that the momentary pleasure of drugs, tobacco, alcohol, or gluttony is deceitful and without value.

- Integrity is what he does when no one is looking. Great men are trustworthy because their secret life is pure and honorable.

Wherever you are on the time line of his maturity, do not take your eyes off the goal for your son. His release day is fast approaching. When that day comes for me, I'm sure I'll stand with tears in my eyes, a full heart of love, and a lifetime of memories. It will be an honor for me to say...

Beautiful son of mine, I have adored you from the very first day. Every day I have praised God for the gracious honor of being your mom. You have been a joy to raise and a delight to love. No smile will ever be sweeter to me than your smile. No laugh will ever move my heart more.

But this day has finally arrived, and a few declarations are in order.

- As from the day you were born, you will continue from this day forward a full recipient of my devotion and my love. No conditions, exclusions, or limitations shall ever be applied.

- Come what may, my support and encouragement for you will remain steadfast.

- I hereby retain and assert my lifetime privileges as the founder and president of your fan club, which basically means it will always be okay for me to cheer the loudest and clap the longest to celebrate whatever you do.

- My advice and counsel remains freely available to you for the rest of your life. But from this day forward, said advice and/or counsel will be dispensed by invitation only, at your request.

- Wherever I am, you and your family are welcome and loved.

- You will always be covered by my prayers.

You have been prepared. And now you are ready. This world needs a great man like you. With my blessing and with great joy, I release you to your manhood. Go into this world and live every day you are given with humility and for the praise of God's glory and grace.

7

A Son Needs His Mom to

Try Sometimes

Her children rise up and call her blessed.

Proverbs 31:28

My sister-in-law is an outdoorsy, athletic, adventurous kind of mom. She can outrun my eleven-year-old nephew every day, all day. She takes him biking and kayaking and zip-lining. And I love her for all that.

My girlfriend down the street is a hip, cool, artistic mom. She always looks amazing, even when you just "drop by." Their home is beautifully decorated with her budget makeovers and their do-it-yourself renovations. She'll paint anything and then change her mind and paint it again. Her photography and artwork doesn't hang in museums, but it sure makes the walls in their home very special.

And then there's the soccer mom I just met who blows me away with her cooking. Everything she makes tastes amazing. But here's the kicker: She presents the food she brings for the guys like she cares. It's not pretentious or too fancy, just thoughtful. Large, yummy desert squares, all cut just so, tucked into a wax paper wrapper and simply displayed on a tray, ready for the boys to grab and enjoy.

Each one of these moms inspires me. I want to be just like every one of them, but the truth is I can't. Each one of those friends was born with a skill set I am never going to have. But what I can do for my boys is try sometimes.

In the seventh grade, Grayson came home from a sleepover and told me about the home where he'd stayed. Back then he didn't have the words to describe what he saw, but what he told me went something like this,

"Mom, at their house, there is stuff hanging on the walls, like every room has pictures and things sitting around and it all goes together somehow. And Mom, can we make our house like that? Like have stuff on the walls, I mean, you know, like more than how it is now."

Are you smiling? I found out later that the mom at the house where Grayson stayed was a part-time interior decorator. We'd talked a few times at football games, but I hadn't been to her home. All I know is, when a thirteen-year-old boy uses a whole lot of words to talk about the décor of his friend's house, moms need to pay attention. How Grayson felt when he walked into their home was more important to him than the particulars of what or why. When I pressed him, he had no idea about colors or style because none of that mattered. Their house felt homey and cozy. And back at home, his mom had IDP. Do you know that syndrome? *Interior Decorating Paralysis*. It's the fear of doing anything to your house because it might be the wrong thing.

Grayson knocked something loose for me that weekend. And not just about hanging pictures on our walls. The more I processed how he felt, the more I realized how many opportunities we have to create those feelings. Some of the feelings I want to intentionally create for my sons are peacefulness, security, comfort, dignity, pleasure, joy, and gratitude. What that means for me personally is not about becoming all things. It's about opening myself up to try sometimes. And learn some new things, even the things totally outside my natural gifting and skills. Here are some of the ways I am trying to create the feelings of *home* for my sons.

Caring about my appearance. Your son may not act like he cares one iota about what you look like or what you have on. If you asked him, he may even say, "Yeah, I really don't care about any of that." But I'm here to tell you he's lying. He's not lying intentionally. He just doesn't know what he's talking about. It will mean something to him when you try with your appearance. I promise. I'm not talking about becoming something you're not, and Lord knows, this whole thing swings the other way when a mom tries to look like a teenager. That is not the plan.

But can you just do a little better, sometimes? If for no one on this earth, for him. Eat a little more healthy. Put on something nice when it's his thing. Ask some cool friend for a new hairdo suggestion. Cover the gray and pluck and shave your legs and use lotion and you know, just try a little more.

William was in elementary school. There was a program in the auditorium and I arrived after the lights had gone down so I quietly worked my way down the aisle in the dark. Afterwards, William said, "Someone came down the aisle and I couldn't see who it was, but I knew it was you because I smelled you. I told my friend, 'Yeah, that's my mom. That's what she smells like.'" Because of that one moment, I wear that same perfume (Lemon Sugar by Fresh) to this day.

Learning to laugh again. When life has been disappointing or tough, our laughter can fade before we realize it's gone. Learning to laugh again was an intentional effort for me. One day I watched my son's face light up when I laughed out loud and caught a glimmer of what just happened in his soul. I wanted to give him more of that feeling when mom laughs.

Throwing the baseball. Many of you moms are sporty girls and boys are your jam. You can rock their sports and I love that. I was a cheerleader in high school and I love dancing. Not a natural boy sport connection. So I bought a baseball and began throwing with the boys when they were little. "Mom, wanna throw?" were some of the sweetest words I ever heard. Of course the day came when a ball landed in my glove like it had been fired from a rifle and our throwing days came to an end. But I still have my glove. Maybe one day a little grandson will want to throw.

I could keep going with more ways to try, but I think you probably get it by now. As the Holy Spirit prompts you about ways to create "feelings" for your son, will you open your heart to some new ideas and just try sometimes?

8

A Son Needs His Mom to

Pull the Car Over

See to it that no one fails to obtain the grace of God;
that no "root of bitterness" springs up and causes
trouble, and by it many become defiled.

Hebrews 12:15

One morning, five minutes before it was time to leave for school, three of my kids looked at the lunch menu taped to the side of the refrigerator and decided they didn't want breaded chicken patties for lunch. I couldn't really blame them. Who in the world would want a breaded chicken patty on a bun? But time was short, and I could offer only peanut butter and jelly sandwiches as a quick replacement. Everybody decided anything was better than a chicken patty, and we began furiously throwing together three sack lunches.

I grabbed the cheese crackers shaped like SpongeBob and filled three snack Ziploc bags, wrapped up some sugar cookies that none of them like, threw in the obligatory piece of fruit that I was sure no one would eat, and passed out quarters to buy milk. We made it. Three packed lunches and still in the car on time.

Grayson, who was in fifth grade and a serious loather of chicken patties, was beside me in the front seat. About the time we got out of our neighborhood, I glanced over at him. He didn't just have that preteen, I'm-grumpy-in-the-morning look on his face. He was mad and on the verge of tears.

"What's going on?" I began gently.

"Mom, this is going to be the worst day ever."

"What do you mean? Did something happen that I don't know about?"

"You gave me the wrong cheese crackers."

"What? There were two boxes, but they're both shaped like SpongeBob. I just used the one that was already open."

"You gave me the Cheese Nips, and the Cheez-Its taste better. Now everything is going to be awful."

Fortunately, I was able to contain the volcanic eruption-type-thing that began happening inside of me. We were driving to school and I've only done this a few times, but that morning, as soon as there was an opportunity, I pulled over to a clearing beside the road for special emphasis. Everyone in the car sat up straight and stared at me while I was pulling over for this spontaneous *Come to Jesus* meeting.

"Grayson, you need to look at me. Cheese Nips? You're going to have an awful day because of Cheese Nips? Well, let me tell you something. If we have an accident on the way to school, that's an awful day. If somebody you love gets sick and goes to the hospital, that's an awful day. If a tornado blows our house away while we're driving to school, that's an awful day. Even chicken patty sandwiches might taste awful, but they cannot cause you to have an awful day. Cheese Nips are crackers. And a cracker cannot cause you to have an awful day. You will only have an awful day because in your mind and in your heart, you are choosing to have an awful day."

I checked the rearview mirror for a quick look at the rest of the children. I looked to see if anybody else needed to be in on this roadside lesson. The three behind me were looking at me with their most spiritual eyes, as if to say, *Oh, Mama, we are so grateful for every cheese cracker we have ever been given.*

We all just sat there, quiet for a moment, letting it all sink in. *Cheese crackers cannot cause an awful day.*

Then I realized I wasn't finished yet. You already know what I said next. In a moment of pure mom genius, I said, "Grayson," (*dramatic pause*) "there are children on the other side of this world who do not have a cheese cracker or a mama to put them in a Ziploc. I just can't believe someone in this family, who has been given so much, could possibly have such an ungrateful heart." Note to our mom selves: The ancient mom things we were never going to say will sometimes just pop right out. Sometimes ancient words still have power, and that's all we can find in the moment. So just roll with it!

As we pulled into the car pool drop-off, all of my kids got out of the car like Chip 'n' Dale. *No, after you. No, pardon me. No, you first.* They all waved and smiled and told me how much they loved me.

But I still wasn't done.

"Grayson, honey, come back for a second." Poor kid shuffled back to the car.

"Grayson, here's how I want you to go into school today. I want you to go to your classroom grateful. This is not an awful day. I want you to bless your teacher. I want you to reach out to the other kids. I want you to ask what you can do to serve others today. And when you get to the cafeteria today, I want you to walk into the room and look at all the kids. As you do that, I want you to ask the Lord, *Who would be grateful to get a bag of cheese crackers today?* Then I want you to give your cheese crackers to somebody with a thankful heart."

Grayson was eleven. I loved him then and now with all my heart. Eleven is a tough time. It's a season of physical and emotional transition and we were like most families, just trying to muddle our way through. But that morning, it was like the Holy Spirit said, *Don't let this one pass. Don't just muddle through today.*

That morning I pulled our car to the side of the road because the lesson had to be underlined. I could not allow a ridiculous frustration to settle in Grayson's soul. His little self wanted to find comfort in annoyance, but I couldn't let that happen. Cheese crackers cannot hijack your day because cheese crackers have no power. We must teach our sons their mind has the power to reject and to choose.

There is a villain stalking our sons. He tempts them with the promise of false comfort. He begs our sons to join him and all the other victims of this cruel world. His ideology is ridiculous, yet so many fall prey. His temptation goes something like this: Choose bitterness when you are disappointed as an alternative form of satisfaction.

Life is never going to be fair for your son or mine. Greater things than cheese crackers will bring a slew of disappointments into their lives. We must do everything we can to teach them how to reject the temptation toward bitterness. Even if it means pulling the car over. And saying some of the mom-things we promised we'd never say.*

9

A Son Needs His Mom to

Teach Him About Collared Shirts, Combed Hair, and Chores

*Owe no one anything, except to love each other, for
the one who loves another has fulfilled the law.*

Romans 13:8

All this used to drive me crazy, but I'm a whole lot better now.

I have the most adorable pictures of my small children, all dressed in clothes I chose for them. Standing together and smiling, everyone has neatly trimmed clean hair and wrinkle-free tucked-in shirts, with nary a frayed seam in sight. They are coordinated and cute, but not too matchy-matchy. Just the way I always dreamed they would be.

Then I discovered two things.

One: God did not give me the color-coordinated, wrinkle-free kind of children. They are not regular children who don't care what they wear. He gave me innovative people who like what they like. And without warning, they have the ability to instantly reinvent themselves, no longer liking the last thing you thought they liked. They are creative, independent, resourceful, philosophical dressers.

And two: A single mom with a broken life and four small kids will eventually have to lay some things down. I mean *down* down. All the way down. Like some things really cannot matter anymore. So please, for the love of everything holy, stop making such a big deal out of little things, because you will die or kill people if you don't Lay. It. All. Down.

Important to note here: You do not have to wait for a broken life to force you to lay down the little things with your children. I promise, some of what I'm getting ready to say can set you free right now. No life drama necessary. Truth is, these lessons were so hard won it would be a crying shame not to share them every time I can. As a young mom, I mistakenly made a big deal out of little things. In the effort to do it all right, I placed too much value on appearances, lists, chores, and rules.

I was wrong.

I grieved my children and I grieved my own heart. When I could finally see what I had been doing, the decision to change was as fast as I could make it. The misguided, uptight mom was not the mom I wanted to be and I never want to live like that again. Here are some of my personal guidelines for the practical things:

- I'd rather lay down the little things in our lives right this second than live in constant upheaval and frustration one more day.

- It's really okay that my kids are not wired like everyone else's kids.

- It's also okay if a system works for another family but doesn't work for us.

- The hearts of people matter more. Keeping their heart the priority means constantly examining my expectations and rearranging when I'm off.

Keeping the heart in mind, I've tried to affirm each son, telling him, *You really do get to like what you like.* Every time it's appropriate, I try to give the freedom to dress the way they like, but with a few boundaries. Here are some of my guidelines about clothes and grooming:

- I require clean. Clean clothes. Clean body. Clean hair.

- They do not get to wear immoral, rebellious, or inappropriate clothes. Thankfully, this hasn't been a battle for us. Obviously, more than the actual piece of clothing, that kind of choice comes from the heart. Before you scream about the shirt, maybe you ask, *Is there something going on with his heart?*

- I require the boys to comply with the school dress code. If the school allows my son's creative interpretation of their dress code, I'm okay with that. If they are required to wear a collared shirt and my son chooses the thrift store Hawaiian print collared shirt and the school says okay, then okay.

- There are times, like weddings and funerals, when the clothes you wear become part of your statement of respect. I've tried to teach the boys that events like that are not about us and it's inappropriate to creatively interpret your attire. For those situations, I require my son to dress with respect for the person and the occasion.

With so few everyday guidelines, that means my sons are no longer color-coordinated. I buy them department store jeans but they prefer thrift store finds. They are more ragamuffin than conventional, but I'll take smiling ragamuffin all day long.

Here is where I finally landed regarding chores:

- Several of my friends used chore charts with their kids, and their charts worked like a dream. For several years after my divorce, my kids were back and forth with their dad, alternating weekends and special occasions. Chore charts became a nightmare for me. The system would fall apart and keeping that thing together required me to become the General Inspector of Everything.

- What worked better for us was building "the team" idea. We're a family and a family works together to care for what has been entrusted to us. Some days that means your brother is off the hook because his exam tomorrow is huge and some days we're all together in the yard pulling weeds, no one excluded.

- My children do not have a chore chart so I had to teach them to step up when their name is called. Then, I had to remember not to call the same name every time! I try to frame my instructions like this, "Grayson, when you get to a stopping place, will you…? William, when you finish reading that chapter, will you…?" There are obviously times I need help immediately, but most of the time I am able to ask in a way that is considerate. What I love now is having one of them come to me and ask, "Mom, when you get a minute, can you come help me with…?"

- I've tried to train everyone how to do everything. And it's understood that no one ever gets too big or too important to do anything. We can all unload the dishwasher or feed the dogs or make something to eat or fold towels or rake leaves. In a family, you never age out of chores.

- When "the team" hasn't pulled their weight, there was usually a family meeting to remind them why we have to pull together. No one can do it all alone. Especially not Mom. My advice is to hold that meeting pre-meltdown and before you are crying so hard you can't speak. Don't ask me how I know these things.

A few years ago, I had traveled to Africa for ten days. My parents came over to help Scott care for everything. The day I returned Scott picked me up at the airport and drove my weary body home. My mom was waiting. Her heart was good and I'm sure she had thought hard about what she wanted to say to me. I walked in the house, said hello, gave her a hug, and then she began. "Angela, you're just going to have to do something about William. His room is a total disaster." And the details of his clutter unfolded. In my weariness, I just listened until she was all done.

I'm sure the Lord helped me in that moment because I replied, "Mama, I totally get your frustration. I've worried about all his clutter too. But then I thought about something. He is a really smart kid who studies all the time. He plays soccer and goes to church and loves God. He is good to me and honest and really funny. He's just a busy, busy guy. I used to worry about his messy room until I remembered something. I knew a high school girl who was a lot like William. Her room was a disaster for at least five years. Do you know what her mom did? It was such a gracious thing to do. Her mom closed the door. That girl turned out okay, don't you think?"

Chores are important, but a word of caution: Care for your son's heart as you implement your plan. And then some days, give him the gift my mama gave me and just close the door.

10

A Son Needs His Mom to

Love His Friends and Make Them Welcome

Whoever sows sparingly will also reap sparingly, and whoever
sows bountifully will also reap bountifully. Each one must
give as he has decided in his heart, not reluctantly or under
compulsion, for God loves a cheerful giver. And God is able to
make all grace abound to you, so that having all sufficiency in
all things at all times, you may abound in every good work.

2 Corinthians 9:6-8

It's Sunday morning and I send my husband on a mission: "Go check around and see how many boys are here." Our boys' friends are drivers, so I'm never really sure if a few more showed up after I went to sleep or if some had to go home. All I know is I don't go looking for sleeping boys. They could be anywhere and what other teenage boys wear for pajamas is information I don't really need. Scott counts the beds, air mattresses, pallets on the floor, and sofas and reports back with a number for the pancake maker.

Years ago, something inside of me broke, or stopped, or got set free. I'm not exactly sure what to call it, because I'm still pretty weird about a lot of things. Being weird is supposed to be fairly common among firstborns, but a random office supply purchase took my weird onto new heights of ridiculous. That was the day the label-maker became my friend. Now, the spice drawer holds identical glass jars, labeled and alphabetically sorted. Hopeful labels stick to the pantry shelves, just in case a family member totally loses his mind and unloads the groceries when I'm not looking. The kitchen cabinets are labeled for vases and candles and such. The linen closet is labeled. And the office, well, you can imagine.

I want the things I'm involved with to be done logically with high standards. I wish we could pause here for a moment to insert a video because here's what you'd see: The people who work in my little office would be standing behind me. And as you read that last sentence, they would begin making faces to get your attention, discreetly trying to give you the head-nod, half-eye-roll look that says, *You. Have. No. Idea.* Makes me laugh to think of them behind me. It doesn't make me want to lower the bar, but it's a good laugh. They would all agree that order and details and beautiful work make me crazy happy.

I'm going on and on about my being weird about order because I'm trying to make a really big point. This is the fine print I don't want you to miss. Loving my sons' friends and all their messy glory is not the mom I used to be. At all. Really.

How one big concrete-truck-sized thing finally broke free in my soul is almost unexplainable.

Except for the grace of God.

From that grace, a new heart of love began to grow inside of me. So much of the old me was broken by divorce, but my heart had remained tightly bound in my orderliness and rules. Then our Father in heaven came to my rescue. His love removed my chains. His presence lifted and carried me. I had known God for a very long time. I had asked His Son to be my Savior. But I had never understood the depths of His love for me. I may never understand all the theology. All I know for sure is that the love of God can set you free.

God's freedom came to me with these instructions: *Give what you have been given. Love like you have been loved.*

Everywhere I go, most people look a lot like me. Messy. I have a feeling you know the kind of messy people I'm talking about. Scattered and unfocused, lost and alone, insecure and too many times improperly labeled by this world. Messy people are a lot like teenage boys. But I am certain that messy people are a lot like this broken, divorced mother of four, who had never understood God's grace was meant for her.

God's grace is meant for you too.

To love your son's friends and treat them like family is to freely give what God has given to you.

Years ago, I told my boys their friends were always welcome in our home. Then I added this: "You never have to ask me again. They can always come over. It's great if you can give me a heads-up when there's a meal, but even if you forget, I'll cut our pieces of chicken in half and add another potato to the pot and we'll make it work." Right now, I'm sitting here trying to find the right words to describe the joy it gives my sons to live in the home with the big welcome mat and the doors wide open. I don't have words because they don't talk about it like that. They say deep things like, "Thanks, Mom." But I just know something special is happening. God is preparing them for even greater things.

Last summer, William helped God test my commitment. Some of his buddies had thrown together an indoor soccer team then entered a national tournament being held in our town. It was one of those tournaments where you lose twice and you're out. The kind of tournament where the other teams had national sponsors. We figured the boys would play two games and be done. Parents didn't even go to the first few games. Game one, they won. Game two, they won again. Game three, winners yet again. I was driving out to a garden center when William called me. "Hey Mom, we won!"

"That's awesome, honey," I said.

Then, in that hurried boy, distracted kind of way, he asked, "Mom, since we won, we have to play again tonight. Can some of the guys come over until the next game?"

"Sure baby," I said. "No problem."

"Hang on a minute," he said. I listened to some muffled talking and a few yells back and forth. "Ummm, Mom, can more guys come over? Like can the whole team just come?"

"Yep, the whole team can come," I said as I exited the interstate and turned my car back toward home. "Are you guys hungry?"

"Oh Mom, we're starving," he said, like it was news.

I hung up the phone with William and called home to Grayson. I told him about 20 guys were on their way to the house. Then I rapid-fired the instructions: *Turn on the oven. Clear off the kitchen counters. Pick up in the TV room. Put the dogs up. Open the front door because they should be there in about ten minutes.* I told him I was stopping at the grocery store and I needed him to help me make sandwiches the minute I walked in.

We fed the team a lot of grilled sandwiches that Tuesday, but here's the part you're going to love. The team kept on winning until Friday night. So most of them stayed at our house. All week. Totally unplanned. Not one boy brought a change of clothes and thankfully I had a stash of Dollar Store toothbrushes. Every game they found enough same-color jerseys to wear and then they'd win again. Friday morning, I asked one of the boys if he wanted to change into some of William's clean clothes while I washed his dirty clothes. I do not lie when I tell you what he said to me: "Nah. Thanks, though. Besides, William has been wearing the same clothes all week too."

You don't have to love your son's friends enough to let them live at your house for a week wearing the same stinky soccer clothes. You don't have to do anything like I've done. But whatever you do will be so much sweeter if you just love your son's friends like God has loved you.

11

A Son Needs His Mom to

Give Him One More Year

*I bless the LORD who gives me counsel; in the
night also my heart instructs me.*

Psalm 16:7

Before my first child began kindergarten, I had the opportunity to talk with two different high school guidance counselors. One worked in the public school setting; the other was a private school counselor. Both of those respected ladies told me something that significantly shaped the education decisions I made for my sons.

Both counselors suggested, if there was any way possible, to give each son one more year at home before kindergarten. They said, "This is more than keeping your son at home because he's not ready to begin kindergarten. We advise the extra year to give your son another year of maturity before college. Going to kindergarten is not usually the problem. The problem comes later, when a boy has completed high school. In high school, he may excel academically or find success in sports, but if he graduates high school still needing another year of maturity, it's too late. The system and his peers will push him along."

Some parents cannot offer an extra year at home for their son. Jobs. Finances. Child care. Health issues. For some families, another year is an impossible consideration. I am still grateful we had the opportunity to follow their advice. Both of my boys had an extra year at home with me before beginning school. Grayson began kindergarten at six years old. William was six and a half. That means this year William is the oldest kid in his high school senior class and we have almost arrived at the reason I kept him home. In seven short months, he'll graduate high school and be on his way to college. Lord, have mercy.

I don't have anything scientific to report to you about my decision. There are no comparison charts or regional data lying around my house. No psychological testing or clinical trials. All I have are my observations and the peace in my heart. Two wise ladies gave advice that resonated with me, so I followed their lead. I believe I made the right decision for our family, but thoughtful explanation has been needed through the years.

Our preschool teachers kindly disagreed with my decision. They said both boys were ready for kindergarten. I agreed with their readiness assessments, but kindergarten wasn't my goal, so I signed the boys up for another year of preschool.

Throughout the years, the main difficulty for us has been navigating the various age and grade divisions for children. Some activities divide children by grade, like school and church. Others divide by age, like club sports. Sometimes I had to make a different call, but generally, I kept the boys with children in their same grade. In recent years, more boys are staying home another year or making the decision to "re-class" along the way, so there are more families navigating the same divisions. Thankfully, we aren't the only "weird" ones anymore.

William was especially vocal for many years, usually saying something like, "I'm supposed to be in *such-and-such* grade, right Mom?" I'd tell him a lot of boys his age were in that grade, but he wasn't *supposed* to be. He was in exactly the right grade. That answer was obviously never impressive to him. Then one day in middle school, he must have said something like that in front of the varsity soccer coach. Thankfully, the coach took the extra moments to say, "William, when you are in high school, that extra year you have is going to be my blessing. I'm glad your mom kept you home." And that was officially the end of William's objection.

Grayson is currently a junior in college and William is finishing his high school senior year, so at this point, I feel like I can give you an honest assessment of the decision to give them another year.

I would do the same thing again, times a million. For my boys and for our family, giving each son one more year at home was hands-down one of the best gifts I could have given.

Again, I feel like I should remind you, psychology may not support this mom's ideas, but it seems to me too many boys aren't given enough years to be little. I think it's okay for boys to have longer to play without a care, unhurried and without stress. The pressure to academically "get ahead" at that age doesn't make sense to me. They have the rest of their lives to get ahead and cram all that learning into their heads. It seems like boys are better prepared if they've had sufficient time to act their age. More time to be silly and creative and just play.

One more year at home was more time for me to give the security of my affection. More snuggles and tenderness and physical closeness. I spent that year keenly aware of the gift we'd been given. There was no way we would ever have that kind of precious time again. If we had not taken the year before kindergarten but decided after high school that our son wasn't ready for college, there was no decision we could make that would bring back the year when he was five. One more quiet year to sit in my lap, to be held when he cried, to be read to and rocked and seen by his mom. Yep, five years old is almost the last of all that.

Back then I hoped an extra year would help satisfy the "little boy" in their souls. More than anything I want them to become strong, mature men, not grown men who still act like little boys. I hoped the freedom to be little longer would have a part in strengthening their maturity later. Some grown men live like they're trying to recover the play they didn't have as boys. Some even seem like they're searching for a woman to mother them instead of partner with them. Call me crazy for making a correlation between a man's strength in maturity and a little boy's first years, but deep in my heart I believe it's true.

Please don't hear me saying, "You have to do this thing or your son is going to become…whatever." That is not my intent, nor is it my heart. The advice we followed was wisdom for *my sons* and without any judgment, I'm sharing our story with you. The longer I am a mom, the more I'm convinced that God has not called us all to parent the same way. His boys are uniquely made. There is wisdom for us as we learn from others, but the greater benefit for your son is that you obey God as He leads.

Listen to God's promptings for you. Study your son and your family. Pay more attention to who he is becoming than the pressure to keep him "on schedule."

In seven months, William will graduate high school. On that day, he will be nineteen years and four months old. I could stop right here and fill the next page with accolades about my boy. But accolades were never the point. Maturity has always been the point. Strength of character is the goal.

It's fall break for us today and the kids are running in and out. Two minutes ago, William came home from a friend's house, grabbed some clothes, talked to me for about three minutes, and then headed back out to practice. It was an ordinary teenage boy moment. William had no idea what I was working on when I looked up at him. The whole time he talked, I searched those brown eyes of his, looking for that thing mamas just know.

Then William headed out the door and hollered back, "I love you, Mama."

The house is quiet again, but my soul is full of assurance. *He's going to be ready to go.*

12

A Son Needs His Mom to

Pray for Great Men to Become His Influencers

Iron sharpens iron, and one man sharpens another.

Proverbs 27:17

At the end of his freshman year, William came home one Friday afternoon and, sometime after dinner, happened to mention in passing, "Oh, I forgot. Chris is coming over to spend the night tonight."

"Chris who?" we asked.

"Chris Kabrich," he said, just like Chris Kabrich was his good buddy who always comes over on Friday nights.

Scott and I looked at each other, obviously thinking exactly the same thing. *He couldn't possibly be talking about the kid we know named Chris Kabrich.* So one of us asked, "Chris Kabrich? High school senior, Chris Kabrich?"

"Yeah," responded Mr. Nonchalant. And up the stairs he went.

There in the kitchen, Scott and I immediately had the same sinking feelings. *Oh, no. William has misunderstood somehow.* Chris Kabrich was only a few weeks away from graduation. He was one of the greatest kids you'd ever want to meet. And one of the happiest. We both felt a little nervous because we knew William looked up to Chris. Chris was a nice kid and all, but we couldn't imagine the "Big Man on Campus" driving to our house for a sleepover at the skinny little freshman's house. The mom in me didn't want William to be hurt. Whatever kind of conversation they'd had, we were sure William had probably misunderstood.

Until the doorbell rang.

And right there on our porch, smiling ear to ear, was the cutest high school senior I'd ever laid eyes on. *Well, I'll be,* I thought to myself, while Chris Kabrich came walking in the front door. He greeted Scott and me with hugs and that fun laugh of his. William came running down the front stairs. Those two high-fived or fist-bumped or whatever. Chris dropped his bag on the floor. "Hope it's okay if I stay over," he said.

Scott and I just tried to act normal.

Chris Kabrich isn't old enough to grasp the powerful answer to prayer he was that night. When he has his own squirrely freshman son, he might begin to understand the huge gift he gave to William. And to me. It was such a big deal for our freshman boy to be seen, and liked, by the senior. And not just any ol' senior—the guy is godly and smart and athletic and funny and cool. He's the kind of influence you pray your son will have.

As amazing and wonderful as you are, one day, your mom-voice will become like white noise to your son. An ever-present hum. An audio book that keeps looping, saying the same things over and over. Your voice is part of soundtrack for his growing up years and after he's heard it all so many times, his head can disconnect from your content. Everything you say, no matter what the content, comes from your voice, with your phrasing and your tone. And it all. Just sounds. The same.

Most of their lives, my kids have traveled with me to speak at women's conferences. But one particular weekend, we drove to Atlanta for a weekend with 4200 teenage girls. My boys were about ten and twelve years old at the time. Needless to say, the whole weekend was a total paradigm shift. There was a lot of squealing and energy and volume and the whole thing was a lot more intimidating for all of them. My boys decided to hang out in the sound booth for safety.

After I spoke to the girls from the stage, I began making my way back to the children. At the same time, Grayson had left the sound booth and was on his way to look for me. We found each other in the stairwell where he ran up to give me the biggest hug. Then with surprise in his voice, he said, "Mom, you're funny." I laughed about his new revelation, "Funny? Grayson, I'm always funny. I was funny this morning while you were eating breakfast. I was funny on the way here in the car. All of your life, I've been funny." But my voice is his mom's voice, something akin to a constant hum.

That day I spoke, his peers laughed and Grayson heard something new. I'm funny.

We cannot take any of this personally. Our sons live with us for a very long time. The very thing that gives them security—our voice—is the very thing that can lose its effect after a while. So moms, pray and ask God to send great influencers into their lives. It's amazing how a college kid or youth pastor or teacher or coach can say the very same thing you have always said. But their voice. A different phrase. A different mannerism. And finally, your son can hear.

Even more, a great man can say things to your son you've never known how to say and give things you would never know how to give. Someone said a boy learns how to be a man in the presence of other men. If that is true, and I believe it is, then moms have to pray for great men to surround our sons. We pray for his dad, his grandfathers, his uncles and cousins to be great men of influence. We pray for cool college guys and sporty athletes and creative musicians who are great men to add their layers of influence in his soul.

These are the years when influence especially matters. We are called to protect our sons and if we have to, moms will kick down doors to remove bad influences. But before we get to the door-kicking, a mom's best defense against bad influence is the distraction of a great influencer for her son.

Ask God to bring great men into your son's life. Be proactive where you can with teachers, coaches, and other leaders. Don't settle for the status quo whenever there is an opportunity to connect your son with someone godly and wise, someone creative and interesting. And don't be tricked into believing you are all he needs. Our sons need great men who will show them the way.

13

A Son Needs His Mom to

Teach Him to Wait His Turn

May you be strengthened with all power, according to his
glorious might, for all endurance and patience with joy.

Colossians 1:11

Long before personal computers and online registration, people stood in line. At the University of North Carolina, we stood in line for everything—precious parking stickers, class schedules, basketball tickets, you name it. After a few years as a student, you'd just walk past a line and assume you were supposed to be in it. The lines wound around buildings and across the quad because the people you were waiting to see never got in a hurry. It could take all day just to drop a class. Changing your major, too big a deal. It was easier to just stick with the one you started with.

There's a funny thing I realized from all those years standing in line. Maybe more than actually getting your turn, being *next* is a really great feeling.

As early as possible, our sons need to be taught that life can be a whole lot like standing in line. You get all your stuff together. Pack a snack. Choose the appropriate path. Muster up your patience. Square your determination. And wait to be next.

A great lesson comes to those who have spent the good part of a lifetime waiting. Sometimes you have all your papers and the necessary credentials and you are in exactly the right line at exactly the right time, but you still have to wait. An agonizing wait. An I-wonder-if-I'm-in-the-right-line wait. A much longer wait than you had expected. All the time, you may be in the correct line, facing the right direction, but your name has not been called because it's just not your turn. Yet.

The lesson of waiting your turn with grace and integrity is the lesson we must entrust to our sons. There's almost nothing worse than encountering a grown man whose mama never taught him to wait.

Someone has said maturity is the ability to delay gratification. As your son learns to wait for the thing he wants so badly, his maturity will increase. If the goal is becoming a man of great character, learning to wait is a lesson we must begin early and weave through all their years. A son needs to understand, if it's something he really wants or the very thing he believes he was made to do, many times in this life, there will be a wait.

We must teach our sons that waiting your turn means…

Trusting in the sovereignty of God. As moms, we can help our sons practice trusting in the faithfulness of God. Talk to him about trusting God. Let him overhear you telling others how much you trust God. Tell him when you are waiting on God for a specific direction or a specific answer. Then tell your son the stories of God's faithfulness to you; your answered prayers. Help him to look to God first. Pray with him about the circumstances that require him to wait. Explain to him that God is the giver of dreams and we can trust Him to keep our dreams safe and protected. As he learns to trust God's perfect timing, a greater patience will grow in his heart.

I love what Oswald Chambers said: "Wait on God and He will work, but don't wait in spiritual sulks because you cannot see an inch in front of you!"* That kind of "non-sulking" waiting is exactly the kind of thing a mom can teach her son.

You can't forget the "yet" part. When it's just not your turn yet, that doesn't mean you are in the wrong line or doing the wrong thing. It also doesn't mean the thing you are waiting on won't ever be. It doesn't mean you're not qualified or that you are headed in the wrong direction. It just means not yet. One of the coolest things about your son deciding *It's just*

---

* Oswald Chambers, *My Utmost for His Highest* (Grand Rapids, MI: Discovery House Publishers, 2009), August 1.

not my turn yet is the freedom it gives him to genuinely celebrate others when their turn comes before his.

It's your time to get ready. When it's finally your turn, wouldn't it be devastating not to be ready? God would say, "Next." And you'd say, "Can I get a few more minutes? I'm not quite there yet." Teach your son how to use the time he waits to get ready! When his name is finally called, he wants to be ready for whatever it is. And when he's ready for his turn, there will be a confidence inside of him that gives him strength.

Sometimes you have done everything you can and you will still have to wait a little longer. Our boys need to know that after they have done everything, prayed, trusted God with a "non-sulking" attitude, celebrated others, and prepared, even then we cannot push or pull God's perfect timing. In times like that, you keep standing on what God has told you to do.

> Therefore take up the whole armor of God, that you may be
> able to withstand in the evil day, and having done all, to stand
> firm (Ephesians 6:13).

As with most strong character traits, there is also a word of caution, a waiting paradox of sorts. In this life, learning to wait patiently for something is a good quality. But spending your whole life waiting for something else is folly. Great men understand the difference. Too many people are waiting to live until they can become something great or until the right person comes along. They can miss their life, waiting for a big break or a big job or a big lottery payoff.

Truth is, from the time they can reason, our boys will be waiting for something. Waiting for dinner. Waiting to go outside for recess. Waiting to be called off the bench and into the game. Waiting to drive. Waiting to date. There will be lots of learning opportunities. But as you teach, don't forget to show him this normal, regular, many days humdrum, wait-a-minute, everyday life is the most precious gift we have.

Living in the joy of this very moment will never require him to wait. Let us teach him both and teach him well.

14

A Son Needs His Mom to

Have a Godly Friend She Can Run Beside

*Oil and perfume make the heart glad, and the sweetness
of a friend comes from his earnest counsel.*

Proverbs 27:9

A few years ago my mentor told me something I've found true for every area of my life. She said, "We pace ourselves according to the people we run beside."

Although the running analogy only applies to my spiritual life, I still like the picture it gives. I am only a runner wannabe. I wear running shoes because they feel great. Nonetheless, any real marathoner can tell you my mentor's advice is true. To run beside someone of like heart and stride keeps you well paced and focused. One runner told me, "I never could have finished a marathon without my running partner. Her constant presence made me more responsible and consistent in my training." My husband is a triathlete and two-time Iron Man finisher who fully agrees. He says the spirit of camaraderie can move you along even when you feel like you have nothing left to give.

So much of my shaping and reshaping as a mom has come from my godly friends. These women who want God's pleasure more than anything have become teachers, sounding boards, counselors, and confidantes. They inspire me to go deeper and to keep searching for the next opportunity to connect with my son or speak truth into his life. They calm my fears and reassure me about all the wacky boy things you don't know until you're a mom.

God has sent some great moms into my life to spiritually run alongside me. Each has come to me in a different season and caused me to run a little stronger. These women share my passion to know God intimately and pursue Him with intentional purpose. They are the kind of women who make me want to get with it and pick up my spiritual pace. These women are boy-mama soul mates. Sent by God to help me look more like Him and less like me and love my sons with a healthy, passionate love.

These words from Gordon MacDonald are full of truth for me:

> I can think of certain people in my world whose company invigorates me, and when they leave, I am full of resolve, ideas, and intentions about God, self-improvement, and service to others. I can also think of people in my world whose presence exhausts me. And when they leave, I am ready for a long, long nap.*

The invigorating women in my life are alive and passionate, always ready to dream, firmly anchored to God and His Word. They raise their sons keeping Christ at the center of their lives and remembering to keep eternity in view.

But there have also been plenty of women in my life who exhaust me.

Many years ago, there was a woman in my life who decided she was going to be my friend. She was a sweet person who loved the Lord, but we lacked a real soul connection. This woman called me almost every day (long before texting and Facebook). Because I was lonely at home with my babies, I began to embrace her as a friend. I tried not to mind that her attitude was usually dismal and depressing. I tried to overlook our divergent theologies. Mostly miserable and sporadic with the Lord, she was the friend who kept coming around. And I just let it all happen.

Over time I began to open up my heart to this woman, until one day she was sitting in my home, giving me very commanding advice about my life. I remember disconnecting from the conversation long enough to think, *Who am I listening to? This is the most graceless stuff I've ever heard. Why am I letting someone who is not passionate about Jesus speak into my life?* I finally woke up and realized that friendship was not healthy for me.

---

* Gordon MacDonald, *Restoring Your Spiritual Passion* (Nashville: Thomas Nelson, 1986), 71.

That person could still be in my life, but I would not give her permission to walk around in my soul.

Proverbs 4:23 says, "Above all else, guard your heart, for everything you do flows from it." Guarding my heart means I must continually ask myself, *Who have I given permission to speak into my life?* I made a commitment to protect my heart because so much is decided there—my attitude toward life, my parenting, my view of the world, and most importantly, my relationship with my Savior.

Deciding to guard my heart forced me to distance my soul from this woman. I had to replace her input with godly wisdom and counsel. I decided to spend less time with her and consciously did not ask for her advice. I began to examine my casual friendships and choose godly women for insight and direction. Caring for my soul meant I had to guard who got permission to walk there.

Who has been given permission to walk around in your soul? Do the friends you run beside spiritually invigorate you to become a better mom? Or do they hinder your walk with God and make you tired? Are there choices you need to make to guard your heart? Is there someone you might run alongside who can help you pick up the pace?

A part of becoming the best mom I can be for my son has been finding another godly mom to make the journey with. God built His church on earth so that we do not have to go it alone. We need the community of other believers and I think that's especially true for moms.

I long to finish well as a mom. I want to be a godly mom all the way to the end. I don't want to burn out and spend the last 20 years of my life in an RV detached from my family, trying to find all the things I think I missed. I want my children to know the blessing of a mom who really loves Jesus and models for them until death the pursuit of holiness and grace.

Having a godly friend to run beside is an integral part of finishing well. Truth is, without those friends, I'd be tempted to quit more often, stay down longer, and give up more times than I start.

Let's encourage one another and run beside one another and run as fast toward the Father as we can. And by the grace of God, that son you are raising will learn about running toward Jesus from his mom. Maybe he'll outrun us all.

15

A Son Needs His Mom to

Stop Waiting on *Perfect* and Do the Best She Can Now

Godliness with contentment is great gain.

1 Timothy 6:6

There is an internal voice inside many of us. Somedays the voice whispers. Other days it yells.

You are not enough.

You're not funny enough.

You're not smart enough.

You're not as cute as those other moms.

Your house isn't decorated.

You can't cook like her.

And on and on and on. The barrage of lies in your head will eventually begin to paralyze the soul. And before you know it, the lies become the louder voice and their seeds of truth take hold in your soul.

After my divorce, all I could hear were the voices. My pain, my disappointment, my failures, my future, my brokenness, and my imperfections. The heartache kept coming and the voices were loud and I did what I've watched many others do. I turned inward. I'm embarrassed to remember my conversations from those years. With both my friends and my family, all I ever talked about was myself. I was just so very self-centered and focused only on my ongoing crummy circumstances.

Obviously I had a lot to walk through, but I was the mother of four precious children who needed their mom to come to her senses. There was a lot going on with me, but mercifully, God eventually made some things clear. Even with all my imperfection and pain, I had to reprioritize my life. The children had to come first. More than anything, they needed me to focus on their hearts and their needs.

What did they need? They needed me to be the best mom I could be. Not perfect, but consistent. Becoming stronger right before their eyes. A woman with a gentle countenance. Lavish with my love. Focused outward, toward them, instead of inside myself, squinting through my pitiful disappointment. They needed me to fall into the arms of God, receive His healing, hear His promises, trust His provision, and then stand up to love them well. Maybe your son needs the same from you.

In those days, one of the greatest hindrances for me was a private, internal waiting game I played. Waiting for someone to come along and rescue me. Waiting for some miraculous intervention to make all the bad things right. All I could think about was myself and my huge responsibilities and all my flaws and failures. I put real living on hold until I could be rescued. Even worse, all that time, my children were put on hold too.

One day it finally hit me. *What if I lay the wishing down? What if I just stop thinking about myself all the time? What if I try with all my heart to love my kids well and build a great life for us? What if I spend my energies doing the best I can instead of hoping something will come along to save us?*

Learning to ignore the crazy-maker voices in my head was a decision that involved three changes. First, I decided to make the children my first priority, turning my outward focus toward them. Second, I asked God to begin the healing I desperately needed on the inside. Third, I decided that even if all those voices and their lies were true, from that day forward my kids deserved better than a mom paralyzed by all her imperfections.

When I stopped waiting on *perfect*, stopped wishing time away and stopped hoping for a different life, it was like my soul woke up and a new tenderness for my kids came rushing in. All of my circumstances stayed the same, but I was changed by the peace that filled my soul.

Deciding not to wait for *perfect* is, to this day, one of the sweetest lessons God has taught me about parenting, especially with my sons. Little boys don't care very much about perfect details. Teenage boys care even less. I would have missed so much about loving them well if God had allowed me to stay in my waiting.

We'd never invite people over if I were still waiting on perfect. Last year I hosted our family Thanksgiving for about 30 people. Sometime in the afternoon I looked to one of side of the room and almost burst out laughing. There were at least 15 different wrong colors of paint making a kind of patchwork quilt on the wall behind our main table. I smiled to myself and thanked the Lord for His grace. I had forgotten those colors were there. In my *waiting on perfect* days, I would have killed myself getting that wall painted before I'd let people come eat at my house. No one cared.

I never would have said we could host 14 semipro soccer players for a week last summer. Are you kidding? Where would that many grown men sleep? Thankfully, free of imperfect, I borrowed air mattresses and bedding and made a wall-to-wall bunkhouse for the guys. They had one and a half bathrooms between them. We fell in love with each one of them. They were happy to be here. And most of all, no one cared.

This life we have is still so obviously imperfect. But I cannot imagine our lives without all the crazy fun we've had and the people we've met and the opportunities to grow. I bless God for the day He said, "Take your eyes off yourself, turn toward your children, and just do the very best you can with what you have today."

Giving up on *perfect* may not be the kind of decision you think it's going to be. Back then I probably would have said I was unwilling to settle, refusing to lower the bar of my high standards. My perfect dreams kept me perpetually waiting to live. They were the dreams manufactured by my insecurity. One day God asked, *Will you trust Me enough to live your life and love your children right now?*

And now I understand more about this gift God calls contentment. Faith in God can help you set aside your striving for perfection and give you the courage to live as best you can.

Dear mom, may the God of contentment make you brave.

16

A Son Needs His Mom to

Be Confident Enough to Lead, Humble Enough to Apologize

*Walk in a manner worthy of the calling to which you
have been called, with all humility and gentleness, with
patience, bearing with one another in love.*

Ephesians 4:1-2

No matter your designation, happily married mom, single mom, remarried mom, or blended family mom, there will inevitably be circumstances that come along and make you doubt your ability to ever be a *good* mom.

No matter how your story has unfolded or why things have turned out the way they have, today, you are the mom of your son. You're the mom. You are in charge. You are the grownup and he is little, even if his "little" is packaged inside a tall teenage body. The authority to parent your son has been given to you. Your story doesn't take away your authority or diminish your responsibility to God to protect, guide, discipline, and lead your son.

My kids' eyes glaze over like a Krispy Kreme doughnut when I say it, but I usually fall back on this one at least once a week: "I am responsible to God for your protection. This really isn't about you or being your friend or what you think in that head of yours. This is about me answering to God for how I have protected you. I don't care if it makes you mad or sad or glad. I am the mom. I will stand in front of God one day, and I'm taking that seriously."

And you know what? It gives my kids a deep sense of security when I stand up and lead with authority. I can see it in their countenances. When

I take charge, I'm not mean or difficult, but I'm searching for wisdom to direct their hearts and maintain healthy boundaries.

When I was a single mom, the kids and I would grab lunch somewhere on Sundays after church. Almost every Sunday, there was a disagreement about where to go. I could eat Mexican food at every meal. Grayson liked stir-fry. The others might chime in about some greasy drive-thru. The after-church lunch arguments exhausted all of us.

Years before I'd told my children the story of their grandfather on Sundays. "You know, my daddy, your Papa, never asked us where we wanted to go after church. We just got in the car and he drove wherever he wanted us to eat. Then we would eat lunch without grumbling. No little kids weighed in about where the best kid toys were. We just went wherever Papa took us and acted grateful. One day I'm going to be like Papa. I'll drive, and you get out and eat wherever I stop."

Another Sunday rolled around and it was the same as usual in the car after church. Then one of the children piped up from the back: "Mom, just be like Papa."

Our sons need us to lead—in the little things like food and in the big things about home and heart. Don't be afraid to be the mom your son needs. Our children need to be children, and that happens when you and I step into our roles with strength and gracious authority.

To lead with confidence means stepping into their confusion with clear, thoughtful decisions, saying no to them when the Holy Spirit tells you to say no and saying yes to them every time we can. Being a confident mom also means we're the first to apologize when we blow it. How will our sons know how to apologize unless we are big enough to model the humility of "I'm sorry"?

I want my sons to realize when they have chosen or acted poorly and learn to seek forgiveness and restoration quickly. We must first model what we hope to teach.

On the other side, when your son says, "I'm sorry," then it's over. There may be consequences, but the offense is over. We cannot berate our children for their mistakes or keep reminding them of their bad decisions. Our tone and countenance must communicate, "It's over." Forgiveness really forgives.

I remember hearing we should treat our family as friends and our friends as family. I believe that's especially true in parenting. We correct, make and accept apologies, and then rebuild tenderness with our children. Their hearts are so precious. No kid should have to endure the pain of grudge-holding or conditional forgiveness. Teach your son how to give and receive forgiveness by the way you give it to him.

Sometimes humility means reversing yourself with your son. Many moms have said to me, "Angela, I have already allowed my son to do such-and-such. How can I say no to him now?" I have learned is that it's very grownup to reverse yourself if you realize you have made a mistake or not chosen what's best for your son.

I have often had to say something like this: "I know I have allowed this in the past, but now I believe I was wrong. I didn't hold a strong boundary for our family. I made a poor choice. But now I know better, so I want to do better for all of us. I realize this may be difficult for you, but I am reversing myself. It would be wrong of me to let something go by when I know it's not best for you or for me. Please forgive me for not doing this sooner or for making you feel confused."

They may grumble or whine, but kids do very well with honesty. I have reversed myself several times after I became better informed or felt the boundary needed to be loosened or tightened in a certain area. To parent in strength means when you reverse yourself, you have to stay there. No slip-sliding away from your newfound wisdom or direction or your son will lose respect for your authority. The last thing you want him to think is, *Yeah, she always says stuff like that, but she never means it.*

It's the godly, confident woman who allows humility to strengthen her parenting. One of the most powerful lessons our sons may ever witness is the example of their mother being prompted by God and changing course as He leads.

May God grant you the confidence to lead your son as you make decisions, no matter the size. May God also grant you the humility to model how leaders seek forgiveness, apologize quickly, and reverse themselves when necessary.

17

A Son Needs His Mom to

Be the Meanest Mom in the World (Sometimes)

Train up a child in the way he should go; even when he is old he will not depart from it.

Proverbs 22:6

In our culture, and in these ridiculous, indulgent times, becoming a boundary-setting mom might just be one of the most difficult things you and I will have to do. Trying to navigate this culture is tough enough. When you add little discouragements, the mom who keeps strong boundaries isn't always the popular mom. Learning to set boundaries for our sons means we'll face times of personal doubt and plenty of opposition from our kids, their friends, and even the parents down the street. And sometimes, when a mom is being strong, she gets "the look." You know the one I mean. It's that squinted evil eye peering across the kitchen table, saying, *You are the meanest mom in the world.*

And then it happens. You have officially become the mom you were never going to be. Back before you had children. Back when you were naïve. Back when you were sure a son could be raised in this world without having to be so "strict."

There is no one way of creating boundaries that will work for every child. Each one is so different. And that makes our job harder, again.

For me, a *rule* is a guiding principle that will not change. Things like, *Do not play ball in the street. Never leave the house without telling someone. Don't open the door for a stranger. Don't cross without looking both ways.*

Toddlers, teenagers, or adults, it doesn't matter. Rules should be the things that aren't going to change.

Boundaries are a whole different animal. A boundary can function in different ways depending on the season of life. A boundary can be like the wall of a prison, ten feet high topped with electrified barbed wire, with patrolling officers keeping guard. Other times, a boundary is like a bungee cord, securely attached but with some room to stretch a little farther if they try. Eventually, as they mature, all of the boundaries can be removed.

We definitely have some rules in our house, but for me, the boundaries require more emotional energy and prayer. Most kids can understand how rules keep them safe. But the boundaries, ugh. Eventually a day comes when your son will believe the boundary about whatever has exceeded its usefulness.

A boundary mom is creating a safe place for her kids to grow up. There are boundaries for their physical safety, their emotional health, and the general, day-to-day creation of good character inside their hearts. We care for their souls, guarding the tender little people they are and the amazing grown-up people they have the capacity to become.

While this whole boundary idea is one of the most important things we do as moms, establishing boundaries isn't actually the hardest part. Maintaining those babies is the thing that can send you right to the mat. It's the day you feel like running from the house, screaming back to your son, "I give up! Just live any way you want. Hope that lazy, rebellious thing works out for you!" But we don't run. We stay in there. And we hold the line of appropriate boundaries. Not because we're trying to be the meanest moms in the world, but because we love them more than life itself.

And those days are so stinkin' hard.

Every time you can, try to maintain your strong boundaries with grace. Being a boundary mom does not mean becoming a legalistic, rule-keeping, ledger-toting, punishment-giving mean ol' mom. I am hoping and praying that what I do to safeguard my children is done with compassion and grace. I talk to them about my decisions to help them understand my reasoning and my heart of love. I have been angry, but I don't make or keep boundaries out of anger. And every time I can make the boundary a little fun, I always try.

But there are always exceptions. When you establish boundaries for your son, you are setting up some guiding principles for the purpose of keeping your family safe. After you've done that, then you have to use your common sense and God-given wisdom to discern when a situation falls into the "exception to the boundary" category. Things happen, situations arise, our sons make mistakes and their moms do too. Sometimes our tenderness matters more than a rigid line. So set good, wise boundaries with great affection. Be willing to be redirected by God and be reasonable with your son.

Then one day, it's time to move the boundary. We use thoughtful boundaries to hold our son back. When it's time, we inch out the lines we've carefully drawn around their potential. One boundary gets a shove when he's old enough. The next one moves because he's finally tall enough. Another one is pushed when he's more responsible. Eventually all the lines are erased and the whole wide world becomes his for the choosing.

Don't be surprised when your boundary is tested. I think kids just need to push up against the boundary every once in a while to make sure it's still there. And truly, I believe it gives them security when they test the boundary and find it's still strong. I will allow a couple of tests, like when my son asks the same question, but in a different way. I'll let him ask twice, maybe three times, but after that I make it clear the testing needs to end. *When you are a trial attorney, you'll make four hundred dollars an hour doing this. But you are not an attorney. You are my kid who is about to step over into disobedience.* It's not a bad thing for your son to test the boundary and encounter strength.

Through the years I've spoken at quite a few teenage girls events. I'll say, "I am going to tell you about some of the strong boundaries I have made around our home, some of the things I am doing to protect my children. When I'm done, you are going to go home, looking lovingly into the eyes of your mom, and say with all sincerity, 'I am so glad Angela Thomas is not my mother.'" The girls all laugh, but I cannot count how many girls have come to me afterward and said, "I wish my mom had been like you. I wish she had been stronger. If she'd just said no to me, even when I pitched a fit and screamed like a baby. My life would be so different if there had been stronger boundaries."

Then there are the moms who slip a piece of paper into my hand that says, "I don't know how to be a boundary mom. Please pray for me."

Moms are protectors. Motivated by love and covered in grace, we establish strong, protecting boundaries because we see what our sons cannot. And if one of those tired days, your son shoots you *the meanest mom in the world* glare, then whoop-de-do. I've been the mean mom plenty of days and not lost one wink of sleep over it.

I'll take safe and protected over being liked. All. Day. Long.

18

A Son Needs His Mom to

Say No to Poker Nights

*Be sober-minded; be watchful. Your adversary the devil prowls
around like a roaring lion, seeking someone to devour.*

1 Peter 5:8

I have nothing against the card game of poker. As a matter of fact, I know
a lot of men who really enjoy it. And all of those men also bet, albeit rel-
atively small amounts, on their playing. But they are grown men who are
willing to pay, literally, for the consequences of their own choosing. They
are also aware, I hope, of the signs of addiction and its devastating effects.

Now, about my sons. I am absolutely certain that while they are still
home with me, my boys do not need any gambling training from other
preteen or teenage boys. Gambling lessons in elementary school or high
school seem ridiculous to me. But one summer day I was surprised about
how many other parents disagree.

I guess the boys were about nine and twelve. They'd been running in
and out of the house with their friends all day. I heard a bunch of boys
come inside then everything got a little too quiet. On my way to inves-
tigate, I heard clinking sounds. *Clink-clink. Clink-clink-clink.* I couldn't
imagine what was making that clinking sound. Then I rounded the corner.
Lo and behold, a casino was being laid out and constructed in my family room. "Hey, guys," I asked in my best non-accusatory tone. "What's
going on?"

"We're gonna learn how to play poker," said one of the boys with a very
straight face.

"You are? Where did you guys get all that stuff?" I asked.

"My dad," a friend of theirs said matter-of-factly while he sorted cards and stacked chips.

Suspicious that they might really be burglars with smuggled poker loot, I asked, "Does your dad know you have all his chips and cards?"

"Yeah. He said I could bring them to your house so we can learn how to play."

"He did?" I wasn't quite sure what to do with that. That boy's dad was a great guy. I was sure his son misunderstood. "Well, guys, I tell you what. I hate to disappoint you, but you're not going to learn how to play poker today."

You can imagine how all that went over. Like a big lead balloon is how it went, in case you can't imagine. My boys acted like they were shocked and I guess they were. We'd never had one conversation about poker. As far as they knew, it was just a game. And it is just a game. It wasn't the game part that bothered me. It was the gambling.

So I called the man, who, I'm grateful to say, is still our friend to this day. I was sure his son had misunderstood his intent. But nope, our friend assured me he'd given his son permission to bring all the poker gear to our house. "But what about the betting?" I asked.

"They're not really betting," he explained. "They're just using chips."

Totally out of my league, I asked, "Don't the chips represent different amounts?"

"Yeah, but they're not actually gambling. They're just using chips, not real money."

Baffled that I was even having that conversation, I said, "I don't know much about this at all, but it seems to me, if the chips represent differing amounts of money, and the whole idea with poker is to make a wager based on your cards hoping you'll win more than you put in, then call me crazy, but it sounds like we're training the boys how to gamble. We're up here discipling future poker players."

He wasn't condescending to me, but he laughed a little laugh and assured me I was overreacting. Said boys learning to play poker is harmless. I asked if he would come to my house and look at the boys to tell me which ones might have a future gambling addiction, and separate them from the ones who would not.

My friend and I agreed to disagree that day. The chips went back where they came from. And I talked to my sons about poker and gambling and why some things may be harmless later, but not now. And I probably said something about preferring safe than sorry. And I'm sure I said something about two sets of good parents believing different things for their children. I had to listen to God leading *me*.

Through the years, we never really expected our parenting values to align with the values of today's culture. I'm not a wack-a-doo or a legalist or a prude, but still, we're more often far apart than aligned. But I must say, I'm continually surprised by the number of times our parenting decisions do not align with the decisions of other respected Christian families.

My intent with our boundaries is to protect our children. Internet. Video games. Cell phones. Television. Movies. Driving privileges. First jobs. There are many divergent opinions about how to navigate our children around all the possible landmines. Even the Christian families many times agree to disagree. As a Christian mom, I have learned that I must listen for the voice of the Holy Spirit. How God guides me for my son may be completely different from my Christian friend's guidance for hers. But God knows my son better than I ever could.

God knows every fiber of my son's DNA just like He knows the number of hairs on his head. God knows what gifts He gave to him. What limitations he might possess. God knows my son's secret struggles, his unspoken dreams, and how best to prepare him for his future.

One of the things these years have taught me is to be respectful of the different ways God leads. Two people can study the same Bible and believe in the same God, yet make different parenting decisions for their children concerning the same boundary. About many things, the Bible is clear and hard to misinterpret. But about some things, the Holy Spirit must lead us with regard to the application. I've been more rigorous about our guidelines for television, movies, and the Internet, waiting later than many of my Christian friends to loosen that boundary. But I must answer to God for how I cared for the ones He entrusted to me.

Sometimes parents thank me for holding firm boundaries regarding an area where they have struggled. Other times, I'm asking another parent to tell me about their decision and why they made that decision for their son so I can better know how to guide my own.

But the most important thing for each of us is to seek God for our boundaries. And be obedient to guide your son as God leads.

19

A Son Needs His Mom to

Teach Him How to Treat All Women

A man who is kind benefits himself, but a cruel man hurts himself.

Proverbs 11:17

A couple of months ago, I posted this question to Facebook: "What do you think our sons need from a mom?"

I had hoped to receive comments that would affirm or deny or elaborate on the notes I'd been making for this project. Not knowing what to expect, I would have considered fifty comments a lavish outpouring of response. You can imagine my shock when the comment counter clicked past 600. Those Facebook friends of mine, graciously, and many times passionately, took the time to write what they think our sons need. I am still so incredibly grateful.

Those 600 comments became 24 printed pages for me to read. I smiled and nodded and laughed out loud the whole time I read them. A lot of the comments affirmed and underscored the same things I believed. What I didn't expect was the number who responded like this:

Moms need to teach their sons…

> *To honor women*
> *To respect women*
> *To care for a woman*
> *To be a gentleman who treats a woman like a lady*
> *How to treat a wife*
>   *their future bride*
>   *a girlfriend*
>   *women in general*
>   *the female gender*

And on and on. My husband read all those comments and said, "A man is supposed to teach them how to do that." My girlfriend said, "A dad is supposed to teach his sons." I fully agree with my husband and my friend: Men should teach sons how to treat women, and many men are doing just that. Intentional men teach their sons and their sons' friends and teammates in homes, churches, schools, and clubs across the country. But our Facebook comments suggest the need is still great. When a man has not been taught how to treat women, the consequences can be devastating.

A mom cannot be a substitute man in the life of her son, but we must do all we can to teach him to treat women well. Women of every age, socioeconomic status, ethnicity, and creed. Teach him that every woman beautifully bears the image of God. As His image-bearer, she is to be treated responsibly, with respect.

Two nights ago I volunteered to help with a high school event in our town. I was the student greeter, assisting the students as they checked in at my table. I knew some of the kids from our school, but most of them were unknown to me. Right off the bat, my student-ministry-love kicked in. I had a blast saying hi to everyone, working especially hard to make the shy girls smile and engage the brawny athletes in a little conversation. My volunteer night moved right along and I felt pretty confident connecting with the kids.

After a couple of hours, three tall basketball players walked in. I said, "Hey guys, I'm so glad you're here." Not one of the three looked at me. Assuming they didn't hear me, I moved a half step closer and tried again, "Hey guys, it's great to see you, just sign right here and head on in." Again, the boys gave me zilch. Not a head nod. Not a blink. Nothing. Nada.

Then why? Why did I do the next thing? I don't know. I guess two hours with hundreds of high school students responding to my hello made me think I should keep trying with those three lugs. So I moved over to where they were signing their names and like a dork said, "You're a junior? Hey, my daughter's a junior. What school do you go to?" Those three boys did not look up or over. They didn't look at each other like a bird had chirped. They never even conceded a yawn. N.O.T.H.I.N.G.

I got nothing from them and as far as I could tell that was exactly their intent. They intended to communicate to me I was nothing.

I guess I'm slow on the uptake. After I realized the boys were being intentional, all my momma-ness kicked in and I thought to myself, *Your moms would lose their minds if they had just seen you act like that. You oughta be ashamed of yourselves. You three don't look like lost orphans who don't know any better. Walking around in nice, clean clothes like you are, you surely have somebody at home who taught you better.*

I can tell you this. I would hear about my son treating another woman like that exactly one time. If he played basketball, he'd better hope his last game was a good one because he might not be seeing that court for a while.

Moms, while we still have them and while we still have the authority to give meaningful consequences, let us commit to teach our sons. Yes, it would be wonderful to have a man teach them, but we must do our part. We cannot sit idly by, wringing our hands.

When your son is young begin using everyday moments as lessons. Let your instructions through the years be intentional and repetitive, weaving threads of character through all kinds of conversations. *One day you'll be a grown man, maybe a husband, and maybe a father. I want you to understand how great men act.*

A great man **does** _____ *because* _____.
A great man **acts** _____ *because* _____.
A great man **says** _____ *because* _____.
A great man **loves** _____ *because* _____.

Little boys can learn to respond with respect when spoken to. Taught to hold the door open for a lady. Recover her dropped paper. Retrieve her coat. Basic kindness respectfully expressed by acts of service. Tell him, *A great man acknowledges a woman with respectful words and respectful actions.*

Tell your dutiful teenage son slogging through his dishwasher chores, *Great men unload the dishwasher because he and his wife are a team. They care for their home together.*

Never allow your son to speak to you with disrespect. *A great man never talks that way to a woman. Even when he disagrees, he chooses respectful words and a rational tone.*

Teaching our sons to respect women involves both his outward expression and his inward attitude. But as your son grows, can I encourage you, as his mom, to give primary concern to his heart? They are going make mistakes and forget what we've told them, but if the attitude of his heart is good, an outward expression will eventually follow.

I decided not to look at the names my basketball boys signed the other night. I didn't want to know. But one had a school jacket, so I e-mailed their coach. I told him I don't know his players' names, because I didn't. Then I relayed our time at the table. No crime. No rules broken. No misconduct or student violation. I don't even think I could recognize the boys again.

I wrote that I hoped one day this coach might have the opportunity to speak into the hearts of his players about women. Not for me; I'm fine. But for their mothers. Their sisters. Their girlfriends. Their future wives. I thought maybe those boys who had been unable to hear my hello might respond to the voice of their coach.

From the speed of his e-mail response back to me, I'd say there's probably gonna be some retraining. May each one of those boys go on to play for the NBA. May they all become a bigger deal than LeBron. And when *Sports Illustrated* does their feature article, I hope the whole world marvels to read about the three great players who also became great men.

20

A Son Needs His Mom to
Teach Him How to Treat His Sister

*And above all these put on love, which binds
everything together in perfect harmony.*

Colossians 3:14

I have two younger brothers, Craig and JT. We grew up in the same house and did the same family things but for some reason, we didn't realize until later that we could have been friends all that time. We weren't enemies or ugly to one another. It was more like we each just did our own thing. As adults, we have become great friends who enjoy one another's company. We look forward to the time we have together and I love them dearly.

After I went off to college, I began to meet families where the siblings not only lived in the same house and loved each other, but had also been friends growing up. That new revelation held some sadness for me. I could have been closer to my brothers sooner.

Before they were born, I began praying for my children to become friends at the earliest possible age. When my fourth baby, AnnaGrace, was born I was beside myself with joy. Even though seven years apart, my oldest, Taylor, would finally have the sister I'd always wanted her to have. But little William was not quite beside himself with the same joy. Two years older, he was never mean to his baby sister. I guess the best way to describe him was "dutiful." *William, can you reach your sister's toy for me? Honey, run and get a diaper for your sister. William, come in here quick and look—AnnaGrace is smiling! Isn't she cute?* He always obliged, but he was less than enthusiastic.

What's interesting is that William was born happy. I mean it, that kid has just been smiling his way through life. But after AnnaGrace was born, his toddler-self would instantly wipe the smile off his face in her presence. If her car seat was on the middle row of the minivan, he wanted to ride on the third row behind her. Sometimes he'd ask before breakfast, "What did AnnaGrace have?" If I told him she chose the sugary treat cereal, he'd choose the high-fiber tree-bark cereal—anything not to be the same. Nothing he did was ever blatant. But it was clear from the start that William had no intention of becoming friends with his baby sister.

So I did what any mom would do. I prayed harder.

I began to ask the Lord to teach me. I didn't have my childhood to draw from on this one. How do you teach a son to love and respect his sister? How does a mom begin to cultivate a friendship between her children? If I know anything about friendship, it's that you can't force people into being friends with each other. Friends choose one another freely, without pressure. Maybe I could teach them how to peaceably live in the same house, but I wanted more for my children. I wanted friendship.

Being the mom of brothers and sisters is a tricky dance some days. One day you're only maintaining a semblance of calm. Other days, one of those seeds you planted sprouts like a dandelion coming from a crack in the sidewalk.

My conversations with the boys about their sisters were lots of times attempts to explain. I wanted them to know girls are different without making it sound like girls are lacking or flawed.

I need you guys to understand that God made your hearts differently. Sometimes boys can say dumb things to each other one minute and act like best friends the next minute. God gave your sister, and all girls, a different kind of heart. Dumb words will hurt her for longer. Her mind will keep remembering what you've said to her. She can even begin to believe your careless words are true. Do not ever call her names and do not allow your friends to do it either.

As soon as they could understand, I told the boys about monthly cycles.

When God created girls, He made a place inside her body where babies are created and grow. Every month, the girls will have a little blood for a few days. There is nothing to be afraid of. That's how God prepares her body to become a mom one day. Sometimes on those days, she might be a little tired or have a headache, but that's all pretty normal. It's an honor to become a mom one day. No boy should ever joke about how a girl's body prepares for motherhood.

If the boys couldn't come to understanding and resolve with their sisters, I gave them one basic rule. In their frustration I'd tell them,

You can be mad at your sister, but sin not. That means she might make you angry. She may disappoint you. You two can completely disagree. But whatever is going on, do not step over into sin. No lying. No screaming names. No hitting. No ambush or booby-traps. No gossip. If you need to go to your room and be alone, that's fine. If you want to talk to me, that's great. But sin not.

Like I told you, I want my boys to have relationships with their sisters that go beyond living peaceably in the same house. I have planted and will continue to plant the seeds I pray blossom into lifetime friendship. Things like...

Shared interests. The boys and girls always had different interests to pursue, but I've tried to find opportunities for all four of them to stand on equal ground. The UNO card game was one of those. The game requires a little skill, but it's mostly a whole lotta luck. We went for months one year with AnnaGrace as the rightful family champion. The baby did something the boys could respect.

Shared struggles. Long before I was a mom I'd read an article about "successful families." The researchers were looking for the common ground in great families. I think something like 200 families from all over the country participated. The only thing all 200 "successful families" had in common was camping. More than the stuff of tents and sleeping bags, camping had given these families shared struggles and shared victories. The time they finally got a fire started in the rain. The tent they had to pitch in the dark.

As much as I wanted to, this single mom never turned our family into campers. But I was deliberate about trying to incorporate the principle. When I traveled to speak, it was many times just the kids and me in our car. We'd set up and tear down and haul boxes and drive back home. There were struggles and victories for *us*. It wasn't camping, but we were doing it together.

Shared affection. As much as I was able, everything about the children was equally divided into four. In every way, I wanted them to understand there were no four kids on the planet loved any more than mine. And each of them was loved exactly the same. From great love for each of them, it was important for each one to feel fairly seen and fairly heard. The boys had to be dragged along to the girls' department and wait patiently. But the girls had to watch while the boys tried on cleats. Their growing up was a back-and-forth that I tried to present to them as "a fair share."

Shared laughter. The day William's stoic heart began to cave was the day he realized he could make AnnaGrace laugh. Her laughter gave him joy. And joy will fix just about anything. He's 18 years old and I think that kid still wakes up every morning wondering, *How am I going to make AnnaGrace laugh today?*

When a boy has a sister, God has given him the potential of a lifelong blessing. As their mom, let's do more than force them to get along. Let's set them up for friendship.

21

A Son Needs His Mom to

Teach Him How to Treat His Wife

*Husbands, love your wives, as Christ loved the
church and gave himself up for her.*

Ephesians 5:25

This topic gives me such a lump in my throat. You know my story. Married. Divorced. Single mom. Remarried. All I wrote was the title, and then I began to cry. So I prayed, *Lord, please come into this room and hold me together. I need to get through this writing. Will You put words to my emotion? Will You bring something powerful from all that's broken? It won't do any good if all I can do is cry over my story. You are my Redeemer. Lord, use me.*

I've hemmed and hawed. Started and stopped. Cried some and then cried a little more. There is a roller coaster of emotion inside of me because I have known both sides.

I have known the pain and brokenness.

And today, humbled by the grace of matchless joy, I know what it's like when a husband loves his wife well.

But we only have a few pages here. Surely there are entire books about training boys to become men who love their wives. In the effort to do this topic justice, I have decided to write a letter to my sons. Like you, I've tried to teach them well. But this thing is too important to leave to their remembering. Just in case they miss something, I want them to have the heart of my guidance in their hands.

When it's time, I intend to add a few more paragraphs to these and slip this letter into my son's hands on the evening before he is married.

In this hurry-up world, I hope there will be a quiet day for you to sit and write your son a letter too. And when the night before comes, with words that probably won't come out right, maybe I'll say,

Well, baby, here we are. Tomorrow's the big day. Since the day you were born, Momma's been trying to show you and teach you and guide you. Now we can see it's all been leading to here. Honey, I love you so much. My heart is full. So proud. So grateful. I'm honored God chose me to raise you. And. Umm. Well. I just wanted you to have this tonight…It's what I've been trying to say all these years…

The beginning of my letter goes like this:

Dear Son,

For so long I wondered how in the world you'd ever learn to love a wife. Don't boys need to see a husband's love in action? Shouldn't they live in a house where love is? See what married love looks like?

I ached for what you didn't have and what I couldn't provide. Our family story was so broken I feared you would end up broken too. The five of us limped along, trying to do the best we could. A little rag-tag single-mom family. You know we didn't have very much back then, but there's something I hope you never forget. When it seemed like we had nothing, we still had the most important thing. Our ragamuffin family belonged to Jesus.

And the years went by. Just us and Jesus.

Then one day in heaven, two holy words were spoken. The authority of those words rocked our world and nothing has ever been the same.

From heaven, Jesus declared over us…*But God.*

> But God, being rich in mercy, because of the great love with which he loved us, even when we were dead in our trespasses, made us alive together with Christ—by grace you have been saved—and raised us up with him and seated us with him in the heavenly places in Christ Jesus, so that in the coming ages he might show the immeasurable riches of his grace in kindness toward us in Christ Jesus (Ephesians 2:4-7).

Because of Jesus, and mercy and the immeasurable riches of grace, our little family was without a husband, *but God* sent Scott Pharr to love us all.

I bless God for sending Scott to show my sons how a husband is supposed to love his wife. After seven years as Scott's wife, I can tell you he walks with wisdom and grace. You'd do well to follow his example.

From Scott I have learned these are some of the ways a great husband loves his wife:

Wake up every day and ask God to be your joy. I cannot fully describe to you the blessing of being married to a happy man.

Start with the beautiful love you have and rekindle that love as often as possible. Tell her about your love. Take her back to the places you fell in love.

Give her the grace God has given to you. As often as you have received it.

Pray with her and pray for her. Study the Bible together.

Pitch in with the little things. You're both on the same team. Take out the trash and unload the dishwasher and fold dry towels.

Learn her favorites and remember them often.

Look at her like you love her. Never stop doing that.

Acquire a bad memory as soon as you can. Forget to remind your wife of all the things she's done wrong.

When she cries, do not walk away. Move closer.

Be eager to talk to her at the end of the day. Talk your decisions through with her. Save some of your experiences to share only with her.

Be her protector, body and soul.

Listen to her. When you feel like you want to jump in with an answer for her struggle, learn to ask her a question instead.

Work with her quirks just like they don't matter. If she leaves the cabinet doors open, become a door closer. If she squeezes toothpaste in the middle, decide you like it that way. If she color-codes your side of the closet, say thank you. Keep the little things little.

Make her laugh sometime every day. And if she should ever stop laughing, work and work and dig and dig until you've found her laughter again.

Share as many things as you can. The best marriage strategy is when the two of you decide to always "double up and do it together." The old saying, "divide and conquer," is the strategy of war.

Be her biggest fan. Cheer wildly from the front row.

In disappointment and defeat, share her sadness and remind her of the hope we have in Christ.

My beautiful son, with all my heart, I pray these two things. May you always be a humble and passionate follower of Jesus Christ. And no matter what blessings your career brings, may your reputation as a husband and father be greater. Be a man who loves his wife and family just as Christ loved and sacrificed for His church.

By God's grace, you are able. Go love her well. It will be my joy to watch you shine.

I love you so,
Mom

22

A Son Needs His Mom to

Help Him Recognize
the Marrying Kind

But as for me and my house, we will serve the LORD.

Joshua 24:15

At this point in the book, I feel sure it's become clear: You are not reading the essays of an expert. I am just a mom trying to do the very best I can. I considered doing a little research for this topic and decided the research wouldn't matter. So let's just assume the son you are raising might possibly choose a wife one day. And let's also assume that having lived in your home for 18 or 20-something years, one of the most powerful influencers in his choosing will be you. Like I said, I haven't studied the psychology, nor do I have any statistics. We may be out on a limb.

But I think it's a decent assumption.

Good or bad. Wise or foolish. Gracious or stingy. The woman you are will guide him. If we hope our son will meet "the marrying kind" of woman, wouldn't it be easier if he has already seen "the marrying kind" in you?

Even if your son is not yet born, there is something you can begin doing today. You can begin consistently praying for his wife. And then pray for yourself. Ask God to strengthen your character and mend your wounds. Ask Him to teach you how to live like Jesus taught.

Right here is where I'm going to pull up for just a second. Maybe nothing in this world has ever really motivated you to change or grow. Not your parents. Not grades. Not money. Not fame. Not even a man. Truth is, God feels so far away to you right now, He isn't enough to motivate you either.

Can I ask you one thing?

But first, if it feels like nothing has the power to motivate you anymore, I want you to know you're not alone. Most everybody I meet, myself included, has taken a pounding from this world. The reality is, most of us are worn out from all the trying and failing. Without the comfort and refreshing of Jesus, few of us would have anything left to give. But what would you be willing to do if you thought there would be more blessing to your son's life? If there's a spark of motivation left inside your weary heart, I imagine that flicker might come from your children. We'll do things for them that nothing else on earth could force us to do.

With all my heart, I hope your love for your son will move you toward God, deciding it's time to become the woman God created you to be. Led by God to create a home and an atmosphere that flows beautifully from your walk with Him.

Sometimes we learn from what has been said to us or the notes we have taken, but more often than not, we learn by sight, sounds, touch, smells. Our sons are no different. The home we are creating, the women we are being right now, is the home that will feel normal to them. The way we speak. What they see us do. When we laugh and when we don't. The scent of hospitality. The presence of peace. The pursuit of joy.

You and I have been entrusted with the honor of building a normal everyday life for these boys. If, when he is grown, he doesn't have to over-come his normal or break free from his normal or defeat the demons of his normal, this everyday life you shape will become his gift. Completely unaware of what's happening to him, the life he lives is quietly drawing a map in his soul. And by God's grace, that map will become a trusted guide. Directing his choices. Steering his heart.

Our sons will instinctively choose "the marrying kind" of woman, more often than not, based on what feels normal to him. Let us be willing to change if we must so our influence can lead him well.

I want the presence of God to feel normal to my son, so I live in such a way as to make God welcome in our home. I pray he'll pursue the heart of God with all he has in part because he has grown up in His presence.

Normal means Bibles lay open. Prayer requests are offered. Church is what you do. God's gifts are noticed.

Normal means we're safe at home. People don't attack one another here. No one has to perform or get fixed up or walk on eggshells. Home is full of peace and acceptance and is the safest place to be.

Normal is the front door always open. When people show up at our home, they're accepted. They may come the first time for dinner, but we hope they want to come back for love. We share what we have because it's the very best way to multiply our joy.

There is a lot of smiling at home. And hugs. And silliness. A smile across the room can bring a lot of hope to the heavy heart. And a little dancing never hurt either.

There are many sounds in our normal, but one is most recognized by its absence. There is no screaming or slamming. Our loud is different.

When I pray for my sons to meet "the marrying kind," I pray she'll bring her personality and her creativity and her quirky things, but with her my son will be able to say to himself, *She makes me feel at home.*

When he's older and it's time I'll probably tell him some of the other things, like...

Jesus is the only one who can save. You need a Savior. You cannot be her Savior. She needs Jesus before she can love you well.

Choose the one who is as much like you in the essentials as possible. When opposites attract, there will eventually be a collision.

You will never make your wife happy. Ever. Before she ever meets you she will have chosen happiness or not. The gift of marriage is the opportunity to add to her happiness.

If she doesn't make you laugh, she is not the girl for you.

If you want to run a six-minute mile, then great, but don't put those kinds of expectations on her. Some things are personal goals and you need to keep them that way. Would you rather have a fast runner or a happy heart? Pay attention to your priorities.

As far as I know, none of my sons will be marrying soon. So the best thing I can do around here is pay attention to God, asking Him to create a beautiful kind of normal in our home. Asking Him to change me. Praying that through us, or in spite of us, by God's grace, our sons recognize the marrying kind.

23

A Son Needs His Mom to

Teach Him That Strong Men Are Compassionate

*Be kind to one another, tenderhearted, forgiving
one another, as God in Christ forgave you.*

Ephesians 4:32

I'm not sure my dad even realizes the gift he gave my brothers and me. On the one hand the gift is a kind of compassion. On the other, it's a slowness to become angry. Daddy never sat down and gave us a lesson. He taught us by weaving his gift into our everyday lives. Even to this day, an interaction could go something like this:

Let's say I am riding in the car with my dad. We're going along just fine until a man pulls into our lane without so much as a glance. We are forced to swerve around the careless driver and I shriek, "Daddy, did you see that man? He scared me to death. He could have hit our car or caused an accident. You need to honk the horn at him."

"Oh, Angela," my dad would say, "that fella wasn't paying attention, was he? Poor old guy. Looks like he's 'bout as old as me. Lost his hair too! You never know what he had on his mind this morning. Maybe his wife yelled at him before he left the house. Or his dog growled at him. Or maybe he's got a bill he can't pay. But he sure wasn't thinking about driving, was he? There's no telling what kind of burden he's carrying today."

Then my dad would laugh. And on we'd drive. And much to my disappointment, there'd be no horn-honking or glaring at the man, who at the very least deserved a scolding.

Grace. My dad is inclined to choose grace. He's not gullible, but he'll usually give people the benefit of the doubt until he has more facts. And while he's handing out grace, he will diffuse the tension by making us laugh. Some of his all-time favorite grace logic includes...

To the grumpy people: "Poor guy was having a hard day. I figured he woke up on the wrong side of the bed. The best thing for him to do is go back to bed and just start all over."

To the happy people: "That woman's so happy. I bet she thought about waking grumpy up this morning, but decided to leave him in bed."

To the mad people: "Whew. Better be careful. You just might sting yourself if don't watch out."

Daddy is not quick to take offense. He recognizes their internal struggle isn't really about him, so he doesn't let the actions and attitudes of others offend him. He doesn't take things personally and he gives a mental grace the other person may never know about.

I'm so grateful I grew up in his house. Lots of people spend years trying to acquire the very gift he modeled for us every day. Many times through the years, a woman has called or written to me and her conversation might begin with, *I hope I didn't offend you when*... or, *I hope it didn't upset you when*... Just like everybody, I've had plenty of reasons to become upset or take offense, but that rarely happens with a stranger or a person I hardly know. My dad taught us to consider their heart before we respond.

When two people don't know each other, they have no history or shared story. Any exchange of critical words or actions originated some other place. I usually assume the critical person I just met speaks from their wounds or their emptiness. While not excusing their behavior, compassionate wisdom helps me respond with greater maturity instead of being drawn into their pain.

A compassionate man might be the greatest paradox this world has ever known. A soft heart. A gentle spirit. A kind word. Some mistakenly associate acts of compassion with weakness. But exactly the opposite is true. Selfish men live indifferent to others' pain. Egotistical men are too stingy to share their concern. A wise man understands compassion as strength.

Not too long ago, I ran across an article by a man named Kozo Hattori. Twelve years of childhood abuse forced him to "act like a man." He writes that the abuse had "wrung most of that compassion out of me by the time I reached adulthood." His article continues:

> Although I was what therapists call "high-functioning," my lack of compassion was like a cancer that poisoned my friendships, relationships, business affairs, and life. At the age of 46, I hit rock bottom. Unemployed and on the verge of divorce, I found myself slapping my four-year-old son's head when he wouldn't listen to me. As a survivor of abuse, I had promised myself that I would never lay a hand on my children, but here I was abusing my beloved son.*

In their book *Raising Cain*, Dan Kindlon and Michael Thompson argue that most boys are raised to be emotionally ignorant: "Lacking an emotional education, a boy meets the pressure of adolescence and that singularly cruel peer culture with the only responses he has learned and practiced—and that he knows are socially acceptable—the typical 'manly' responses of anger, aggression, and emotional withdrawal."†

As moms raising boys, we must teach our sons differently. They have to understand compassion is a characteristic of strong men.

A strong man leads with compassion. He recognizes the importance of first impressions, but doesn't jump to conclusions without the facts.

A strong man is slow to anger. When a man's first inclination is to give the benefit of the doubt, the acceleration of his anger is slowed.

A strong man is not easily offended. His strength comes from understanding the person who takes no offense receives the greater benefit. Giving a moment of grace instead of raging with anger saves him time, steadies his blood pressure, frees him from additional stress, and keeps him focused instead of chasing distraction.

A strong man is merciful. He understands the human nature is flawed and people all over the world need a Savior. Mistakes are made.

---

* Kozo Hattori, "5 Habits of Highly Compassionate Men," *Yes Magazine*, April 2, 2014, http://www.yes
  magazine.org/happiness/five-habits-of-highly-compassionate-men.

† Dan Kindlon and Michael Thompson, *Raising Cain* (New York: Ballantine Books, 1999), 5.

Unintended words are spoken. But compassion gives the gift of grace it has received.

A strong man doesn't tease about things that cannot be changed. People cannot change where they are born. The height they are given. The parents they have.

A strong man is smarter than foul language and coarse words. His mind is more creative than the lowest, basest terms our culture has given him.

Raise your son to be strong. Raise him to be compassionate.

24

A Son Needs His Mom to

Believe He'll Come Through the Fog

When I was a child, I spoke like a child, I thought like a child, I reasoned like a child. When I became a man, I gave up childish ways.

1 Corinthians 13:11

Grayson was somewhere between 13 and 14 years old when, unbeknownst to me, a thick fog rolled in out of nowhere. Before I realized what was happening, something irresistible and magnetic lured him in. With a dense haze between us, I could barely trace the image of my bright and beautiful son anymore. My heart knew he was still there, but the fog hung so thick, many days I feared he was gone.

How can something as ethereal-sounding as fog hold an adolescent boy hostage?

I had no answers then. I still don't understand it now.

All I know is that every single day, I hated the fog for taking my son. And every single day, my heart felt like it would surely break.

I've tried to think of a better word than *fog* to describe this adolescent boy phenomenon. But *fog* still seems the best word. Just like a cloud that makes bright lights grow dim. When this whole thing started with Grayson, I hadn't seen the scope of what we were facing. I remember thinking he was just acting a little weird. Tucking William into bed one night, younger than Grayson by three years, William promised, "I'm never gonna act weird like Grayson."

"Good idea," I told him. "*Weird* makes things harder than they have to be." At the time, I had no idea the fog that makes you weird is nearly unavoidable.

William intended to make good on his promise, but a day still came and the fog settled on him. But try as he might, all his good intentions and a determination not to be weird could not overcome the pull. The years of haze and blur came to him too. Thankfully by then, I understood the fog is not forever.

Here's how one article describes the situation:

> Scientists used to think human brain development was pretty complete by age 10. Or as [neurologist Frances Jensen] puts it, that "a teenage brain is just an adult brain with fewer miles on it."
>
> But it's not. To begin with, she says, a crucial part of the brain—the frontal lobes—are not fully connected. Really.
>
> "It's the part of the brain that says: 'Is this a good idea? What is the consequence of this action?'" Jensen says. "It's not that they don't have a frontal lobe. And they can use it. But they're going to access it more slowly."
>
> That's because the nerve cells that connect teenagers' frontal lobes with the rest of their brains are sluggish. Teenagers don't have as much of the fatty coating called myelin, or "white matter," that adults have in this area.
>
> Think of it as insulation on an electrical wire. Nerves need myelin for nerve signals to flow freely. Spotty or thin myelin leads to inefficient communication between one part of the brain and another...This also may explain why teenagers often seem so maddeningly self-centered. "You think of them as these surly, rude, selfish people," Jensen says. "Well, actually, that's the developmental stage they're at. They aren't yet at that place where they're thinking about—or capable, necessarily—of thinking about the effects of their behavior on other people. That requires insight."

And insight requires—that's right—a fully connected frontal lobe.*

At least there's a scientific explanation for the fog, but I'm not sure understanding the science helps any of us know how to live through it. Both my boys have years before they'll reach the age of fully closed synapses, but each of them is on the other side of the fog. I hope some of my fog-coping strategies will be helpful to you.

If boy fog is in your forecast, begin to prepare your heart. Being a little prepared is a million times better than the devastating day your happy boy leaves for three years, and, oh yeah, the whole world forgot to tell you it might happen. Also, boy fog forecasting is like your local weather report. If they say there's a good chance for rain, take your umbrella. If you don't get rain, then yippee, you didn't need it. Prepared is good.

Remember Charlie Brown's friend, the Peanuts character Pigpen? A cloud of dirt and dust followed him everywhere he went. Well, that's kind of how I came to picture my boys and their fog. It just went everywhere with them. When I saw myself outside the swirl of their fog, I could understand my role more easily. Guiding. Watching for things the fog had hidden. Like Pigpen, my boys had no idea this whole fog thing followed them everywhere. One day William was so annoyed he put about ten words together, looked up, and asked, "Mom, why do you keep saying I'm in a fog?" The adults in the room gave each other the look. *Poor guy. He has no idea.* And he didn't. They truly don't get it.

When inefficient brain connectors or fog or whatever began to distance my boys from the rest of the family, I tried to give them their space. But I wouldn't let them be "gone." Even if they just stared through dinner, grunted one-syllable words, and slurped a little, they had to be there. Even if the door to their room is closed a lot more. It's okay—you can still knock and go in.

I'm sad to tell you, boys are prone to lose their smiles in the fog. I tried not to stop smiling just because they did. It's an act of love to keep smiling

---

* Richard Knox, "The Teen Brain: It's Just Not Grown Up Yet," *NPR*, March 1, 2010, http://www.npr .org/124119468.

at your son when you just want to cry. Or hold yourself together when you get so mad, you just want knock a smile back on that smug little face.

You should know the fog has superpowers. Crying or screaming or knocking a son's head off will not lift the fog. So try not to waste your good emotions on any of that.

Their eyes will make you sad too. And this one hurts like crazy. When the little boy twinkle leaves for a while, their empty eyes seem to shout, *You are the dumbest woman on earth.* Don't believe any of it. Boys in a fog are the dumbest people on earth, not you.

Being lost and confused when everyone else in the family knows what's going on is the byproduct of fog. Reduced visibility means you only see yourself. Only think about yourself. It's a never-ending dilemma. Try to get your boy to look out and squint through the fog long enough to see there's a great big world still going on all around him. Just try not to kill him. Did that sound harsh? When he's engulfed by the cloud and only thinks about himself, give me a call. Don't hurt him.

I have a picture of William and his cousins. Seven children are properly sitting on the sofa by birth order. William is upside-down, standing on his head, smiling like a sneak. Since that kid was born, he was filled with joy. When he went into the fog, I'd show him that picture sometimes. "That boy is still inside of you and one day he'll be back," I'd remind him. Never stop believing he'll make it through.

And last, some days it feels like the fog takes the best mom strategies and renders them powerless. But there is one the fog can't touch. Your prayers. Start praying now and keep praying. You will need God's wisdom and he will need God's grace.

Here is the very best news. Those boys who walk into the fog come back to you. How will you know? One day he'll accidently smile without trying. Another day, his burst of laughter will surprise you both. Then one night, he'll run into the room to ask you something and you'll catch a glimpse of the twinkle.

And your boy will be on his way back.

25

A Son Needs His Mom to

Teach Him How to Ask a Girl to Prom

In humility count others more significant than yourselves.

Philippians 2:3

The spring of his junior year, Grayson decided to invite a sweet girl to prom. A few years before, he'd made some intentional decisions about not dating, so going to prom that year was more about being part of a fun high school tradition. He asked a beautiful girl from our church. They were in the same big friend group. She was fun and easy to talk to and interesting.

Then he told me how he asked her to prom. I can't remember the details of the whole thing, but it was some kind of appointment for coffee where he spent way too long talking about what going to prom did not mean. There was no special, fun invitation. No pizza with pepperonis that spell PROM? No balloons to pop for the invite. No scavenger hunt. No serenading guys behind him. Nothing creative or fun. Just a stinky old meeting to "talk" about going to prom.

After I heard all this, I said, "Grayson, that was awful. You're gonna need to go back and do that whole thing again."

"What do you mean? I just didn't want her to think it was something more or meant something it didn't," he responded honestly.

"Honey, I'm surprised she agreed to go. That whole thing sounds more like a business agreement than a prom invite. I understand what you wanted to communicate, but in the process, you drained every bit of fun from the room. You're supposed to be creative or at the very least steal an invitation idea from some other guy."

"But Mom, I didn't want it to be a big deal."

"Well, mission accomplished. But here's the thing. I think you could have said the part about going as friends and even the part about no future dating intentions but still kept the actual invitation fun and lighthearted. Girls store memories in ways you can't yet understand. And those memories, good or bad, shape places in their hearts. I want you to be responsible enough to speak to a girl honestly, yet not press your point so hard that it unintentionally wounds."

I don't think Grayson ever worked up the guts to re-ask her to prom, but I sure think he heard me that day. He was new to asking a girl to do anything. I wanted to make sure he understood girls hear in different ways. She will be more inclined to listen with her heart. My sons need to speak from that awareness.

Moms have to teach their sons about the hearts of girls. They have a responsibility to act and speak with kindness, not just with a girlfriend or close friend, but with all the girls in their life. Sometimes that means paying attention to the content of their words. Other times it means paying attention to the message of their actions.

Several times I've asked one of our boys about a girl who dropped by or talked to me after school. Many times I'd get the old, "She's great, Mom. We're just friends." And depending on what my "girl instincts" told me, I might have to ask him, "Does she know you are just friends? Have you said anything that might send another message?" I realize people can jump to all kinds of conclusions over the littlest things, but I want my boys to be responsible enough to try and communicate well, whether in word or in deed.

Our son Storm was invited to attend homecoming at another school. In his mind, he was trying to be nice to the girl who invited him, but never really answered her with a yes or no. Two days before the big dance, the unsuspecting girl dropped by our house to give him a bowtie. I wasn't at home at the time, but evidently he said he hadn't planned on going and she left in tears. All I knew was it sounded awful. The next morning my phone rang as I was boarding a plane to leave town, so I texted my husband with its message and the flight attendant closed the door.

By the time I landed on the other side of the country, the homecoming-bowtie misunderstanding had been handled. Evidently, after straightening out the facts, Scott drove to the florist and ordered a corsage. Then he called Storm to tell him he was going to homecoming. And he made one more declaration: Not only would Storm be attending homecoming the next night in his bowtie, but Storm was also going to make sure his date had a good time. Scott explained when you allow a girl to believe something false because you're too cowardly to tell her the truth, then you have essentially lied to her. He also told him that's not the way we do things. The heart of a girl is too valuable.

After all that, I'm not sure his date had very much fun—and who could blame her? But Storm said he tried, and I was proud of him for trying to undo all the mess he'd made.

Having been a teenage girl and also being the mom of two girls, I want my boys to be considerate and kind to the girls they will meet. I want them to understand their responsibility to be thoughtful to all women—not just girlfriends or close friends. That means not chiming in when little boys say dumb things about little girls on the playground. As they grow older, it means standing up for the honor and protection of women and girls. Holding doors and other acts of kindness that communicate respect and basic decency. To everyone. Especially the one you believe feels unlovely.

Tell your son that when the whole gang goes to Wendy's after church, it's his job to make sure the girls "on the fringe" are invited. Teach him how to communicate a yes or no to a girl with kindness. Tell him saying hello to a girl doesn't mean he "likes" her. He can say hi to people. Be nice.

I still smile about Grayson treating his prom invitation like a contract negotiation. His mom had warned him to take special care with matters of the heart and he didn't want to do anything to hurt his good friend. But I must have forgotten to tell him a clear communicator doesn't have to be a killjoy.

Maybe we'll have girls and communication straightened out before it's time for any of them to get down on one knee.

26

A Son Needs His Mom to

Lay His Sports on the Altar of God

*If then you have been raised with Christ, seek the things that are
above, where Christ is, seated at the right hand of God. Set your
minds on things that are above, not on things that are on earth.*

Colossians 3:1-3

Among all four children, someone has played almost every sport under the sun. After all the years, all the signups, the tryouts, practices, equipment, and tears, one sport finally emerged at the top of our family giftedness. The beautiful game of soccer.

As little boys, William and Grayson both played soccer. Grayson went from soccer to middle school baseball, then lacrosse, then football, finishing out high school running cross country and track. William has stayed with soccer, but many times it was soccer and something else. Soccer and baseball. Soccer and basketball. Soccer and track. Eventually soccer won out and took its rightful throne as the king of sports in our house. We really do love the sport.

But me, the weirdo mom, made a mistake about one thing. I assumed we, the parents of sporty people, were all on the same page. The page that says, *Soccer is a sport, not a god. We play the game of soccer for lots of reasons, but it does not give us life. We enjoy so much about the game, but it cannot be our joy, nor will it ever be.*

I don't know where I was the day somebody decided parents should assist their little boys in building an altar to their chosen sport. An altar where the son would subsequently lay his heart and make sacrifices and bow down to worship every day.

I was not on the same page.

In the spirit of factual retelling, no coach or program, as far as I know, has ever alluded to altar building or the worship of soccer gods while instructing my son. But it almost doesn't matter, because this thing I'm talking about is bigger than a man or a program. The delusional obsession with our sons and their sports is a phenomenon on the verge of swallowing an entire country of well-meaning people.

Did you hear me earlier when I said I love soccer? And not just soccer—our whole family just loves sports. Participating. Watching. Talking. We love going to games and cheering and high-fiving all the way home. One of the best days all year is our annual huge Super Bowl party. Everything about sports can be so much fun.

But what's going on with youth sports these days seems to have fallen off the bridge of fun into a rushing river of insane. Our youth sport-crazed culture feels legitimately scary to me. I feel sad for the athletes and I feel sad for their parents.

I recently met a mom at a women's event who talked to me about her 18-year-old son's recent poor performance with his sport. Then she went on to tell me about all the tactics she was using to force him to achieve the goal. And the threats. And the calls from his other relatives to "tell him to get it done." She finished with this: "It's just all in his head. I know he can do it."

I nodded my head and agreed with her assessment. It sounded like her son was a great athlete, just not performing at his previous ability. So I said, "Sounds like you're right and it's all in his head." I understood her desire to see her son step up and do the very thing she knew he could do. But it sounded like this kid had been taking a pounding. So I added, "Whatever has him defeated in his head, just make sure it doesn't go to his heart. It's just a game, after all. If his heart is good, everything's gonna be okay."

She looked at me like we had just become strangers. Those last few sentences may as well have been spoken in Swahili. We were no longer speaking the same language.

This year's NCAA statistics* report that...

---

* "Estimated Probability of Competing in Athletics Beyond the High School Interscholastic Level," NCAA, September 24, 2013, https://www.ncaa.org/sites/default/files/Probability-of-going-pro-methodology_Update2013.pdf.

3.3 percent of high school basketball players will play for an NCAA institution.

0.03 percent of high school basketball players go on to play professionally.

6.5 percent of high school football players will play for an NCAA institution.

0.08 percent of high school football players go on to play professionally.

5.7 percent of high school soccer players will play for an NCAA institution.

0.09 percent of high school soccer players go on to play professionally.

What these statistics, and more just like them, tell us is this: Investing exorbitant amounts of money and time into a sport hoping to receive an athletic college scholarship is statistically a poor investment. Do high school players receive amazing athletic scholarships? Yes, they do. Is it likely your son or mine will be one of them? Around five percent of our sons are going to college with a sports scholarship.

I've definitely never been one to let statistics scare me away from anything. Besides, they have to give those scholarships to somebody, right? It might as well be my son or yours they give them to. But I also want the statistics to guide me toward wisdom. And wisdom says the odds are even lower if…

- my son is good at his sport, but not a stand-out hitter, runner, or scorer.
- my son is good at his sport, but his heart's not in it.
- my son is good at his sport, but loves something else more.
- my son flat-out hates the sport, but his parents and coaches keep demanding he play.

Around ninth grade, our really good soccer player, William, began to love academics more. He still had all his soccer gifting, but his heart had changed. He loved the coach and the team. He wanted to perform well when he was there. But in the off hours, his heart became more interested in science than soccer. Rather than spending money on a soccer coach to "get him back on track," statistics and wisdom and good old common sense told us to spend money on an SAT tutor. William will always love soccer, but it's more likely he'll be helped through college by his other interests. At that point, it would have been downright dumb to continue pouring into soccer like his college dreams depended on it.

I totally understand how parents can jump from the bridge of having fun into the river of insane obsession. The pressure is almost unreal. As a young player, William had a gift. Other coaches and parents could see it. After a while, the onslaught of pressure to make him a big thing was over-whelming. It scares me to think how easy it would have been for us to buy in. No one would have blamed us if we had spent the past ten years of his life "chasing the dream."

I had to lay William's soccer on the altar of God. If God gave him the gift then God would show us what to do with it. Through the years that has meant many things:

- When a club tournament was scheduled the same weekend as our church youth retreat, I would let the coach know well in advance William wouldn't be there. Every coach I've ever spoken to understood. Sometimes you will have to throw down your mom card. The mom card trumps everything so that a son can be taught some things matter more than his sport.

- When William was younger and seemed consumed with soccer, I told him over and over that I loved his skill but his heart and his mind and his academics mattered more. Even if he became the greatest player in the world, he needed to know those things would always be more important. I couldn't let the order get rearranged.

- When he still loved the game but decided to love academics more, I knew he was making the right decision. Then he quit

playing club ball to pursue other studies and I felt a little sad.
The weekends with other families had become part of our life,
but I couldn't push William to stay with the club when his
heart had obviously told him something different.

- When he didn't start a game his entire senior year, I was
  forced to examine my own heart. I realized I had wanted his
  name called at the start for me. He had long ago decided he
  wanted academics more than a starting run time. I had let his
  place on the field define me. *For the love. How embarrassing.*

If I could encourage you to do one thing, it's this. Lay your son's sport
on God's altar. If he is to be the next Heisman trophy winner, God will
guide you. If he needs a little more training, God will lead you. If it's time
to take another path, He'll show you. And all the while, with his sport on
the altar, you can trust our sovereign God to use that sport as He wills. To
shape. To challenge. To discipline. To inspire.

Cheering from the bleachers is one of the most fun things moms do.
So hold it all with open hands. Kneel before God and never let the culture pressure you to bow to the sport.

Then get yourself to all the games and have the best time ever!

27

A Son Needs His Mom to
Make Church Non-Negotiable

*And let us consider how to stir up one another to love
and good works, not neglecting to meet together, as is
the habit of some, but encouraging one another, and
all the more as you see the Day drawing near.*

Hebrews 10:24-25

This year marks 24 years for me.

I have been learning how to be my kids' mom for 24 years. I'm glad I still don't feel old enough to have children that old. But at the same time, the peace with which I write to you affirms 24 years have passed.

Through the years, with God's grace and my parents' influence, I've gotten a few parenting things right. But with other things, I've tripped and stumbled and many times had to humble myself and change my ways. What I'm writing about today is one of those things my parents gave me. Without their model, I'm not sure how I would have known about the importance of our children being in church.

So as I write to you today, please hear my compassion. If someone didn't model a commitment to church, how would you know? I don't write to beat you up. I write with the conviction and assurance 24 years brings. And I write to tell you it's not too late.

Since the birth of my first child, two commitments have proven to be the most important and best decisions I have made as a mom:

First, to submit myself to the teaching and leadership of Jesus Christ. He is my Savior, but He is also my guide. His wisdom instructs me as a parent. The indwelling of the Holy Spirit convicts and directs my heart. In the moments I have stumbled onto exactly the right answer or path for one of my children, I am convinced beyond all reason, those anointed moments were not of my own doing. Without hesitation or doubt, I can tell you every right thing I've done has come about because of God's Spirit in me and through me.

The second most important decision was keeping church a non-negotiable for our family.

The wording on that second decision looks pretty harsh. *Non-negotiable.* But non-negotiable is exactly what I mean. Our family attends church and that's a commitment I'm firm about keeping. But also I've learned a gracious mom is able to make firm decisions and see them through without acting like a ruthless dictator.

In our family, we go to church. We go to church Sunday mornings and midweek. We go to small groups and Bible studies and prayer times. We even go to extra things like concerts and potlucks and cleanup days. When we moved to this town, we chose a church where Jesus Christ is worshipped and His Word, the Bible, is taught with integrity. Then we bought a house close to our church. From the very beginning, we understood the other people attending our church were just like us, sinners who have proven they need a Savior. All of us on our way home. None of us yet perfected. So there will be good times and lean times, victories and discouragements, but come what may, we're committed to our church. We cheer for the other churches in our town, but we don't have to jump around, looking for what we might be missing. We long for the depth of relationship only connected time can bring.

I could write an entire book about all the ways being part of a church has shaped my life, but for sake of brevity...

- Church in my youth gave me a sense of community and acceptance that remains to this day.
- Church in college challenged me to know Christ more.
- Church in seminary was the place where academia met reality.
- Church as a staff member was the opportunity to give what I'd been given.

- Church as a young married was the sweetest community of grace this new mom had ever known.

- Church in my divorce was counsel, protection, healing, support, and hope.

- Church in my new marriage is the place where the redeemed begin again.

- Church as an older mom is the circle coming back around with community, acceptance, and instruction for my children who long for more of God.

- We're not there yet, but we hope church as empty nesters is the place where we will serve and give until the end.

No matter where I've lived or the season of my life, church has consistently been the most profound instrument of God in my life. So I take my kids to church. It's a non-negotiable.

I want you to take your son to church too.

When he's little, packing that diaper bag might be a hassle, but start taking him to church as soon as you can. The blessing will be his and yours. If your family stays in church, a day will inevitably come when your teenage son would rather sleep in. This is exactly where the non-negotiable part comes in. You tell him that's what Sunday afternoon naps are for and you roll that boy out of bed and keep on taking him to church. And youth group too!

I understand this culture doesn't take kindly to strong opinions, especially when those opinions involve God. Neither do our contemporaries believe we should "force" our beliefs on our kids. I can promise you this: Keeping my kids in church is not forcing them to believe. You can't force anyone to believe anything. Every one of my children must eventually choose for themselves. They will decide whether or not to trust in the Jesus they've encountered at church. Which is exactly why you must choose a church centered around the only One strong enough to save. To spend 18 years learning about "good things," or going week after week to hear about a man building his own kingdom, is to rob them of the opportunity to know both the love and the grace of our Savior, Jesus.

If this whole idea is cramping your style, let me just go ahead and push you right over the edge. Several years ago, we decided our family was even going to go to church on vacations. One Sunday, we probably looked like a rock band filing into the pew of a little mountain church. We were dressed in vacation clothes, but we were welcomed and we worshipped nonetheless. Another Sunday, we arrived as strangers in a tiny coastal church but left so connected both to God and those kind people. Another Sunday, it was Easter morning and our family worshipped Jesus at the Hillsong Church in Paris where the presence of God bridged culture and languages and moved us to tears. Over and over again, going to church wherever we are on vacation has been a beautiful lesson for our family about the fellowship of believers and the presence of God the world over.

Being non-negotiable about church means it's what we do. Church is part of our family culture.

Maybe you have been more wishy-washy than committed, but God is prompting your heart to make a change for your family.

I'll leave you with my sister-in-law's story. Laura is the single mom of four boys. She has always taken them to church. But as the boys got older it was easier to let it slide sometimes. Soccer games. Schoolwork. Who could blame her? It's all too much for anybody, much less a single mom.

After the two older boys had gone to college, she told the two younger high-school-aged boys they were going back to church. They were going to go to worship services and Sunday school and youth group and whatever else they had. She said all of them were going all in. You can imagine the boys' lack of enthusiasm.

But Laura was non-negotiable. They went to church every Sunday. And every Wednesday. The boys would drag themselves in behind their mom and go to their class because she said they had to. For weeks.

And one day, those boys met God. Each one made his own intellectual choice to believe, but Laura's firm decision to keep them in the presence of God and in fellowship with God's people was such a beautiful strong decision for their souls.

And when those smart, creative boys met God, everything changed. Every. Single. Thing. Her third son just left for college last week. He's attending a private Christian college that costs more than the state school.

But he begged to go. And earned the scholarships. Because he wanted to go to college with other believers.

More than anything on this earth, I want my sons to walk with God. To know Him by name. To live in His love and for His renown.

I am non-negotiable about church because I want my family in the presence of God. I want my sons to have every opportunity to know Him and love Him as Savior.

28

A Son Needs His Mom to

Stand at the Front Door

Do not neglect to show hospitality to strangers, for thereby some have entertained angels unawares.

Hebrews 13:2

We have an open-door policy in our home, mostly because I think it's the way Jesus would have us live. The boys have our permission to bring their friends over most any time, and one of the things Scott and I want to communicate to their friends is a genuine happiness to have them in our home.

Years ago I read a study about the brain and joy. Apparently there is a place in your brain that produces a chemical to give you the experience of joy. That "joy center" is triggered by many things, but is highly activated when you walk into a room and the people in that room are happy to see you. We want folks who come to our house to feel joy.

A son needs his mom to stand at the front door to welcome the world of friends he'll bring home.

When Grayson was in high school, I think he brought home every international student they had. We had a blast trying to bridge the languages and cultures. The night he brought Marco from Bologna, Italy, home, of course I was making spaghetti. Marco's English wasn't so good, so he smiled a lot. But I'm pretty sure when I invited him to stay for dinner he knew I was apologizing profusely for the spaghetti he was about to eat. We laughed and loved on Marco that night. Our sons need to understand hospitality as one of the beautiful ways the love of God is extended through us to others.

What began with welcoming a few kids at a time must have given us more courage. Through the years we've tried to open the doors wider and wider. We host a Super Bowl Sunday with whoever can come and last year, Grayson brought 20 kids home from college. "Oh, Mom, is it okay if ten of them spend the night?"

"Sure baby, if they don't mind sleeping everywhere," I said.

"They don't mind," he said. "They're just happy to be in a home."

Last year, we offered to host the potluck for our soccer team families. It was August, so I told them to bring lawn chairs. We can't fit all those people inside, but in the yard, there would be plenty of room. That night it rained nonstop, so over a hundred people had to come inside. I just pushed everything out of the garage and opened the front door anyway. One of the sweetest memories of my mom life was watching the team bus pull in front of the house and then all those boys running through the rain to come inside. After everyone was fed and packed in like sardines, I glanced out the front door. Now I wish I'd taken a picture. All the boys had taken off their muddy cleats and thrown them into a huge pile on the porch. *Lord, I don't know how You piled them all in here, but thank You for this muddy, crowded blessing.*

We stand at the door to welcome. Then, sometimes, a mom needs to stand at the front door to give wisdom.

One hot summer day, lots of kids from church had been swimming at the neighborhood pool. I guess they decided they'd had enough sun, so home they came. The boys in wet swimsuits wrapped in towels arrived first. Then came a carload of girls. They were good girls who just weren't thinking. Five or six of them began to file out of one car. All of them cutie-pies. All of them in bikini swimsuits, no towels. I was standing at the front door when they came toward me, waving and smiling. I knew this might not go over too well. "You are the cutest girls ever," I said.

"Thanks," they responded in their varying higher-pitched girly gig-gly way.

"Hey, I don't want any of you girls to be offended. You are all beautiful and wonderful girls. But I'm going to need you to put something over your swimsuits before you come in. There are a lot of teenage guys inside, so can you just run to your car and find something to pull on?" That was not their happiest moment. But they all found something else to wear and came back where I hugged them and welcomed them inside.

Then sometimes a mom stands at the front door to receive the lesson.

One afternoon a bunch of guys rolled in. I knew some of the boys that day, but there were a few I didn't know. One of the new boys plopped onto a stool in the kitchen and I began to ask him all the usual questions. *Where do you live? What do you want to do after high school?* And so on. I'd talked to this kid for about ten minutes and I'm not really sure how to say this next thing. I was thinking, *The boys have brought a bad kid into this house. This guy is arrogant and self-serving and he's probably doing bad things. I don't like this kid and I'm thinking he should not be here.* After our conversation, I was pretty eaten up with anxiety over this boy. I talked to the boys about him later and then ran the whole conversation past my husband. I was pretty certain the kid was sketchy with bad-influencer potential and decided he needed to stay away. Mama-bear was riled up.

The next morning I had been reading my Bible and praying and eventually my prayers turned to the sketchy boy. Just as I was getting ready to ask God for His protection, something broke in my spirit. It was like I could hear the Lord asking me, *Angela, whose house do you want Me to send him to? Where exactly do you suggest this boy go to hear about Jesus?*

I was stunned. And quiet. *Here,* I eventually answered. *Lord, please forgive me. Send him here. We'll tell him about Jesus.*

My next conversation was with my sons. Humbled by God, the only way to start was with, "Hey guys, I'm sorry." I went on to explain what had happened in my prayers. And what I felt like God said. I told them to bring that guy back. This was the place for him to meet Jesus.

A son needs his mom to stand at the front door to welcome his friends and protect him from foolishness…and then sometimes she stands there to learn.

29

A Son Needs His Mom to

Be His Advocate

As he passed by, he saw a man blind from birth. And his disciples asked him, "Rabbi, who sinned, this man or his parents, that he was born blind?" Jesus answered, "It was not that this man sinned, or his parents, but that the works of God might be displayed in him."

John 9:1-3

All moms are called to be champions who advocate for their sons. With one hand, the advocate-mom keeps a firm grasp on reality. She sees the reality of her son's limitations and his struggles and doesn't run and hide from his needs. With the other hand, an advocate-mom puts hope in a chokehold. Ever searching for her son's good. Ever believing in his potential. Ever praying for his best.

From the moment I began praying about this book I had my friend Carla on my mind. And not just Carla. There is my sister-in-law, Jodi, and our nephew, eleven-year-old Cole. My Texas friend Amy and her son, Jack. So many special women in my life take the role of advocate-mom to a depth of commitment like I have never known. They are each moms to sons with special needs. And they are truly my mom-heroes.

In the eighth grade, Carla was the cute new girl at our school. I'm not exactly sure how it happened that year, but somehow the new girl and the nerdy girl became great friends. From then until we graduated high school, Carla was my car pool buddy and fashion icon and the best encourager a girl ever had. Different colleges took us down different paths until we eventually lost touch. But five years ago, God returned Carla to me. After thirty years, we picked right up like nothing had changed. But lots of things had changed for us both. We were both moms. We had both been single moms with struggles and pain. But the most profound change happened when a diagnosis changed Carla's life forever. Her oldest son, Nick, was autistic.

Nick is now 25 years old and a college graduate with an honors degree in biology. Because of his struggles, Nick probably won't know until heaven what kind of woman God chose to be his mom. I have never in my life met a more committed mom. She became an advocate for Nick before anybody knew what an advocate-mom was. For 25 years, she has fought and cried and prayed to make a way for her son in this world. I'm so proud of who she is and wanted to share her with you. Carla inspires me to be a better mom. I hope she inspires you too.

Carla, how early did you notice something with Nick was not as it should be?

By the time Nick was two and a half, my mom-radar was going off. When I mentioned some of my concerns to our pediatrician, I was told, "He's just a boy," and he made me feel silly for mentioning anything. I was pregnant at the time and tried to let it go, but the next months became even more worrisome. I decided to begin writing down my observations and my questions. At Nick's three-year check-up, I took my list to the appointment, and just like he'd been cued, Nick had a huge meltdown in the office. My list plus Nick's meltdown were finally enough to convince the pediatrician to send us to a specialist.

How did you get a diagnosis for Nick?

The head of pediatric neurology at UNC Chapel Hill diagnosed Nick with ADHD and Pervasive Developmental Disorder. A speech therapist told us Nick's speech was approximately 18 months delayed. The UNC TEACCH Autistic Program is where we learned Nick was autistic.

How did your husband respond?

My husband was supportive in that he went to all of Nick's initial evaluations and appointments. He also paid for the therapies he needed, but that was about it. My husband couldn't accept that there was something wrong with his son. His family also ignored Nick's disability. Nick's diagnosis wasn't the reason our marriage ended, but it certainly played a big part.

What does being an advocate-mom mean to you?

To be an advocate-mom means never giving up, no matter how many times the answer is no. When Nick was young, there wasn't much information or access to options like today. You couldn't Google answers from the Internet. I basically read every book I could get my hands on and called everyone I could find to ask questions about how to help him. You really have to be persistent to learn all you can about your child's issues. From kindergarten through college, it's a fight to get the services he needs. Depending on your son, being his advocate can continue after his schooling is finished. Trying to discern his adult needs and get answers for his future. Is he able to work? Does he qualify for disability? Are there special services in your city? Where will he live? The questions for advocates never stop.

When did you get to stop being Nick's advocate?

As you know, an advocate-mom never stops. Even now, at age 25, I'm trying to discern what's best for Nick. I'm still gauging what he's capable of doing for himself and when I need to step in and help. As an adult college graduate, there are very few services still available to him, but this advocate-mom keeps searching for options.

How did Nick's struggles affect you personally?

This is a hard one. I don't think I fully know how Nick's struggles affected me because I spent so many years in "survive and fix it" mode. I got up and did what I had to do every day. One time, when he was small, prediagnosis, I did think I'd cracked. My husband worked 70 to 80 hours a week, so I was always alone with the kids. I had a colicky newborn and a traumatizing three-year-old with undiagnosed Autism and ADHD. It was unbelievably stressful. One night I ended up in the corner, curled up on the floor, rocking and numb. I was finally broken. Somehow the next morning I got up and moved on. I had to. At some point, I had to let go of all of the dreams about what my child's life would be like. Even now, it still breaks my heart when I think about how difficult things have been for Nick. It's still hard to see him struggle with the things that are simple for others. I do believe that God made Nick just exactly as he is supposed to be, exactly how God wanted Nick. I don't understand why and I don't have to. I find comfort in knowing God doesn't make mistakes. God has a plan for Nick and loves him just exactly as he is. That's pretty amazing to me. It's hard to care for yourself when your son requires so much, especially when he's young. But you must take care of yourself. You have to take a break from the situation to recharge so you can keep moving forward, being the best mom you can be. It's also hard to let others help, but we have to. Sometimes we feel like no one can take care of our son like we can. That's probably true, but at the same time, you must take a break and welcome the extra set of hands from time to time.

If you could only give one piece of advice, what would it be?

My advice to advocate-moms is never quit. Whether your son has special needs or not, just don't quit. No matter what. Listen to your gut because that's where God tells you how to pay attention to your son. Keep pushing until you find a way to meet his needs. Don't let others dissuade you from what you know is right for him.

30

A Son Needs His Mom to

Make Him Do a Few Things He'd Rather Not Do

*Do all things without grumbling or questioning, that you
may be blameless and innocent, children of God without
blemish in the midst of a crooked and twisted generation,
among whom you shine as lights in the world.*

Philippians 2:14-15

My boys have already been to more women's conferences than any man should be required to attend in a lifetime. They've had to wait patiently behind book tables. Meet more cheek-squeezing ladies than they can count. And truth be told, there were probably times they forced themselves to smile and say something nice when all they really wanted to do was run outside and kick a ball. With a bunch of boys. In a field of dirt.

And here's the truth: I haven't ever felt one pang of sympathy for either of them about all the women's events they've had to go to. As a matter of fact, I think it's good for kids to do a few things they don't want to do. That lesson is called, *Welcome to Your Future Life.* One day, they'll be glad their mama made them practice obedience and being nice and wearing clean clothes to things. And for the love, it's not like I dragged them to the honky-tonk every weekend. We've been with the Lord. And His loud, crazy, teary, fun ladies.

When the boys were eight and ten, I'd been invited to speak to the ladies at First Baptist Church in Atlanta. It was an evening Christmas event. For some reason, the girls were doing other things and only the boys traveled with me that night. When we arrived at the church, the room where we were meeting was decorated for Christmas, everything twinkling and lovely. But the room arrangement was just a bit unusual. The book table was at the front near the platform. From where I was going to be teaching, just to my right, there was a draped table that had been stacked with my books.

The boys played and scurried around until it was almost time for the meeting to begin. The church had offered several options for them during the meeting. They could go into a room close by to watch a video. There was also a college girl who had offered to take them to the gym. I bent down to ask them what they'd like to do,

"Hey guys, we're about to start. My part will only take about an hour. Do you want to go watch a video, play in the gym, or just quietly sit in the back of the room?"

"We want to stay under there," they proposed, pointing toward the book table.

"The table?" I laughed, like they intended to be funny. "I have to talk for an hour. That table is in front of all these ladies. If you go under there, you'll have to stay the whole time. And you'll have to be completely still. And quiet." I was sure my response had correctly addressed their inattention to the details.

"We know. But we just want to be up there." The puppy-dog eyes of the schemers looked up at me.

"What are you going to do lying still like a statue under a table for an hour?" My time was running out and I needed to quickly convince two little boys of their potentially disastrous idea.

"We have our Game Boys and we'll put them on silent." At that moment I realized their under-the-table proposition had been a while in the planning. My strategists were prepared for all the regular parental objections.

Thinking back, I still can't believe what I said next. "Okay, let's go. We're about to start and I've got to get you guys under that drape."

So I put two happy clams underneath the book table at the front of the stage. Checked the silent switch on their games. Kissed their goofy heads and walked over to take my seat. For the next hour or so, I watched that table from the corner of my eye, expecting, at any moment, to see the whole thing flip and two boys come running to me with a squabble. So I talked. And then I prayed. And finally I said, "Amen."

I opened my eyes and looked over at the table. Nothing moved. *Ahh, I bet they've fallen asleep.* Eventually making my way through the ladies, I bent down to raise the table skirt, and there were two of the happiest, smiling faces you've ever seen. They hadn't been asleep at all. One long look into their eyes and I could have melted right there, on the spot. My love for them was so intense. The joy of being their mom was almost more than I could hold in my heart.

"You guys are amazing," I said, and I meant it. "Were you about to lose your mind under here waiting for me to finish?"

"Mom, it was sooo fun," said the two-man debate team, thrilled to have just proven their great idea worked.

Through the years, there have been plenty of opportunities for the boys to creatively survive another place or situation requiring obedience in the face of great boredom. They haven't always been so creative and many times, I'm sure they were bored to tears. I have tried to be gracious to them, understanding and grateful. I would reward them with something like "a swim at the hotel pool when this is over." But I've also tried to teach them boring comes with the journey. It's okay to be bored sometimes.

Some days you just have to do what is required. It might be boring. Not where you want to be. And nothing like what you'd rather be doing. But sometimes, what you want doesn't matter.

We are a family and we're living this life together. We make sacrifices for one another and we're going to do it with respect. We support one another and show up for one another. What it takes to be a family means every one is not always doing their most interesting thing. Sometimes when you do exactly the right thing, you're just gonna be bored. And this will be the way it is for the rest of your life.

If you can learn to find joy, even in those moments, you will be blessed. But even more, your lives will become blessings for others.

My new mom friend, do not be misled. Our sons need their moms to train them how to do things they'd rather not do. Not with a grumpy, resentful obedience, but with grace. Like most everything that really matters, this practice begins with me. When I am inconvenienced with grace, they see. When I am bored, yet kind, sitting through yet another T-ball practice, they will feel it.

Let us show them with our grace how to give their time and their presence. This powerful lesson will serve them for a lifetime.

31

A Son Needs His Mom to

Show Him the Truth About Superlatives

For by the grace given to me I say to everyone among you not to think of himself more highly than he ought to think, but to think with sober judgment, each according to the measure of faith that God has assigned.

Romans 12:3

Our family is smack dab in the middle of three high school senior years in a row. Last year was Storm. This year is William's turn. And next year, our grand finale will be the high school graduation of Anna-Grace. Lord, have mercy.

About this time of year, students are nominated and the votes are cast. When the ballots are counted, the senior class will announce to great fanfare their Senior Superlative Awards. You remember those, don't you? The Most Likely to…The Best All-Around…The Biggest…The Superlative Awards are fun, kind of like a pat on the back from your class.

Just like your children, all of my kids have been getting superlative awards since pre-K. I have boxes and boxes, labeled with each child's name, filled with award papers and pins, newspaper clippings, music programs, sports letters, academic certificates, and on and on. We might possibly have some kind of recognition for almost every little thing they've ever done. My attic can testify.

This is William's senior year, so my focus is intentionally on him these days. People have come to know William in many ways. He's William, the smart kid; William, the soccer player; or William, the funny guy. On top of how he is already known, this year will finish with all those awards, the Senior Superlative Awards, his Academic Awards, his Service Awards, and his Athletic Awards. Then he'll graduate with all those papers and labels and certificates and stuff, put them in a box in the attic and head off to college.

I'm trying to pay attention while this year is happening, because as much as I love to celebrate, I don't want William driving to some university next year believing he is the sum of all the stuff in those boxes. Those boxes are filled with the records of what he has done. Those papers are not his identity. Those gold stars and diplomas and awards are his accomplishments. But William is so much more than what he has done.

I need my son to understand the truth about superlatives. Superlatives are compliments you have earned. Those accomplishments and all their glory will become your college résumé and one day, they might even become your press release. I do not want William to diminish what he is able to do with the life God has given to him. But I also do not want him confused. *What he does* and *who he is* are two different things.

About this time next year, William will be sitting in a dorm room somewhere. The guys on his hall will still be unfamiliar. The boxes of his awards will be collecting dust in the attic. No one will know how smart he is, or how accomplished or how crazy funny. If his identity is based on the past, or what people know of him, or his circumstances, the loneliness of that dorm room will just be the beginning of more disappointment to come. When all you have is what you do, then you have to make your accomplishments known in order to be somebody. But what if no one sees what you do or how great you are or the value of your work? What if your plans fail or you make mistakes or your body breaks?

If no one sees, or if you can no longer *do*, then what are you?

You are a man with a mistaken identity. Confused. Disappointed. Lost.

My pastor, Don Miller, says we must base our identity on what cannot and will not change. He says too many people think,

What I do determines who I am.

But the Bible teaches,

Who I am determines what I do.

The person who doesn't know Jesus,
>*Does so he can be.*
The one who follows Jesus,
>*Does because of who he is.*

We must teach our sons about their true identity so they can live in the strength Christ provides. The glory of their superlatives will fade, but their hope in Christ cannot.

Teach your son about his identity from the Bible. Show your son what it looks like to build a life based on your identity in Christ. I hope these statements from Neil Anderson will be helpful to guide you.

According to the Bible, if you are a Christian, these statements are true for you.*

I am accepted…

John 1:12 – I am God's child.

John 15:15 – As a disciple, I am a friend of Jesus Christ.

Romans 5:1 – I have been justified.

1 Corinthians 6:17 – I am united with the Lord, and I am one with Him in spirit.

1 Corinthians 6:19-20 – I have been bought with a price and I belong to God.

1 Corinthians 12:27 – I am a member of Christ's body.

Ephesians 1:3-8 – I have been chosen by God and adopted as His child.

Colossians 1:13-14 – I have been redeemed and forgiven of all my sins.

Colossians 2:9-10 – I am complete in Christ.

Hebrews 4:14-16 – I have direct access to the throne of grace through Jesus Christ.

I am secure…

Romans 8:1-2 – I am free from condemnation.

---

* Neil Anderson, "Who I Am in Christ," *Freedom in Christ Ministries*, https://www.ficm.org/handy-links/who-i-am-in-christ.

Romans 8:28 – I am assured that God works for my good in all circumstances.

Romans 8:31-39 – I am free from any condemnation brought against me and I cannot be separated from the love of God.

2 Corinthians 1:21-22 – I have been established, anointed and sealed by God.

Colossians 3:1-4 – I am hidden with Christ in God.

Philippians 1:6 – I am confident that God will complete the good work He started in me.

Philippians 3:20 – I am a citizen of heaven.

2 Timothy 1:7 – I have not been given a spirit of fear but of power, love and a sound mind.

1 John 5:18 – I am born of God and the evil one cannot touch me.

I am significant…

John 15:5 – I am a branch of Jesus Christ, the true vine, and a channel of His life.

John 15:16 – I have been chosen and appointed to bear fruit.

1 Corinthians 3:16 – I am God's temple.

2 Corinthians 5:17-21 – I am a minister of reconciliation for God.

Ephesians 2:6 – I am seated with Jesus Christ in the heavenly realm.

Ephesians 2:10 – I am God's workmanship.

Ephesians 3:12 – I may approach God with freedom and confidence.

Philippians 4:13 – I can do all things through Christ, who strengthens me.

32

A Son Needs His Mom to

Know What to Do When He's Afraid

*Blessed be the God and Father of our Lord Jesus Christ, the
Father of mercies and God of all comfort, who comforts us in
all our affliction, so that we may be able to comfort those who
are in any affliction, with the comfort with which we ourselves
are comforted by God. For as we share abundantly in Christ's
sufferings, so through Christ we share abundantly in comfort too.*

2 Corinthians 1:3-5

William is my third-born child. I have called him the party since he was born, because wherever he goes, he brings the party. Maybe it's his third place in the birth order, but no matter the reason, I'm thankful William is an easy, happy-go-lucky, kind of boy.

For lots of years we called him Renaissance because he loved (and still does) so many things. As a little boy he would be in the classroom all day, stay late for soccer, and run to the car with a tenor sax in one hand and soccer bag in the other. From the back seat, he'd swipe my phone to check the stock market and tell me how many shares of something he should have bought the day before.

But up until age 12 or 13, my little Renaissance man struggled with one particular fear. William was afraid of being alone. He has grown up in a big family with lots of people, so he never really had to be alone. And as brave and smart as he has been about everything else, I'll never forget my sweet William telling me being alone just made him feel afraid.

One morning I needed to leave for the airport around eight. The kids were out of school and everyone was away with a friend except William. The night before I left I asked, already knowing the answer, "Do you want to sleep in tomorrow morning? Or do you want to get up and go with us?" Without hesitation, he said he wanted to get up early. He just didn't like to be alone.

One day I was praying about William's fear when I realized my deep desire to love him well is almost nothing compared to our heavenly Father's love for us. Everything this fallen mom longs to give to William as a parent, God already possesses in perfection and offers freely to those who call Him Father. As I sought the Lord for guidance with William's fear, these beautiful steps of theology kept taking me higher and reshaping my heart.

- I wanted to love William well when he was afraid, so I sought the Lord.

- In the seeking, I came to understand so much more of our Father's love for us.

- And when I knew more about God's patient lovingkindness toward me, I longed to give like He gives.

I sought the Lord for William, but first, our kind Father comforted me. The truth of His character soothed my fears and removed my worries. I took deep breaths in His presence. His promised peace calmed my anxious heart.

These next principles are first for you. Let their truth give you peace and remove all your fears. Then, turn and give God's truth to your son.

God is not mad at me when I feel afraid. He knows the limitations of our humanity. He created us with earthly minds and emotions. He is not mad when we come to him with our fears. The Bible says God has compassion on our weakness. He wants us to come to Him.

I am not mad at my son for being afraid. He is a boy, not yet a man, and I am his mom. My heart is filled with compassion and there is no anger, no teasing, no belittling, and no tests to make him prove he's tough when he's not.

I do not have to be afraid. God is here. Scripture says God is near to the brokenhearted. Our heavenly Father promises to give us the comfort He knows we cannot find apart from Him. He is present. He is our refuge. Our safety. Our hiding place.

When I sense my son is fearful, I go to Him. William was a born snuggle-bunny. Hugs made him feel safe. Just as God runs to comfort me, I do the same for my own son. God never makes me prove I'm tough by leaving me alone in my fear. Neither would I do that to him.

There is nothing I can do to remove God's love for me. Romans 8 says there is nothing that can ever separate us from the love of God—not our fears, not our trembling. Not even our confusion about the heartaches that come into our lives. We cannot ask, "God, where are You right now?" and push Him away with our cries.

There is nothing William could do, no fear he could have, that would make me love him less. I will not always understand his fears or his decision or his motives. But as a mom who longs to give what I am being given, there is nothing he can do to change my love.

One thing I am sure of: God sees me and He sees you. He knows my fears before I can name them. As I receive His comfort and His rest for my soul, then I will have the comfort and rest of God for my son.

A Son Needs His Mom to

Bring a South African Home

*Above all, keep loving one another earnestly, since
love covers a multitude of sins. Show hospitality
to one another without grumbling.*

1 Peter 4:8-9

In high school, our family's name was added to the list of soccer families, and early one summer day there came an e-mail. The varsity coach
had written to ask for two host families in the fall. He was making plans
for the arrival of two new international students, both of whom would
be joining the team.

I read that e-mail and thought, *I love that our coach brings these boys to
our school. It's great to be in the soccer family now and hear about what's going
on, but nope, we cannot host anyone in our home.* Delete.

About two weeks later, a different version of the same e-mail came to
us again. *Yep, it's still a no-go for us.* Delete.

In a few weeks, there was a phone call from the coach to William. He
came downstairs and said, "Mom, Coach wants to know if our family can
host an international student."

"Baby, I just don't think we can. You know your grandmother is sick.
I'm not sure if I'll need to spend more time with her or go back and forth.
Not this year, honey. Maybe next year."

A few days later, the same e-mail arrived again, but this time even more
urgent. Two boys were on their way. *We just really and truly cannot. For the
third time, no.* Delete.

At dinner that night the third e-mail came up and we all talked about
it again. The kids understood our dilemma. There was no way our family

could commit to a boy. We wouldn't be able to him give our full attention. We had a very long list of logical and legitimate reasons it was not a good time to be a host family.

When Scott and I got to our bedroom that night, one of us said, "I guess he could sleep in the bonus room. When my parents are in town, they will still have the guest room." And so the conversation began. By the time we fell asleep, we'd decided to set aside our list of good reasons, surrender to the nagging, and do something that made absolutely no sense. *All right, already. Good grief. We'll take one.*

The next day Scott called the coach and told him, "We'll take one." Coach told Scott we'd be getting the boy from South Africa. His name was Storm. When Scott got off the phone and told me the news, I said, "Call that coach back and check to see if he has a different boy. Ask him if he's got a boy with a different name. Maybe he's got a boy named Peace. I don't need a storm in this house," I whined.

The very next day we drove across town to pick up our new son, Storm.

We didn't plan on falling in love with him, but we did.

We didn't plan on hanging his senior picture on our wall, but it's there.

Storm's mom passed away when he was a little boy and he came to us at 17. He was about six foot one at the time, and all soccer muscle.

He'd lived with us about six weeks before he came into the kitchen and said in his proper Queen's English, "I feel weird calling you Angela."

"Well, honey, what do you want to call me?"

Long pause. "Mom."

"Well"—my turn to pause—"why don't you try it out and see how it feels?"

Yesterday, his text to me read, *I love you, Mom.* With all we had going on at the time, I didn't know there was room in my heart, but there was. I love Storm too.

The coach asked us to host Storm for six months. This coming summer will be three years since I became an African mom. He doesn't live here every day anymore. In the fall, Scott and I drove him to New York to begin college. He's playing soccer there, so we watch his games online and text most days and send care packages and make sure he gets his flu shot. Just the regular family kind of things.

The truth was, we did not have room in our lives to add one more teen-age boy. God had to nearly break down the door to bring that child into our home. Then about a month after Storm came, my parents moved in. They fell in love with him too. When my mama went to heaven, Daddy asked Storm to join the other grandsons as a pallbearer.

It's been a crazy few years with our Storm. Our family is better for it and I pray he is too.

You may not have room in your house or your heart to host an inter-national student. Believe me, I totally get it. The past two summers, I've spent my fair share of e-mails trying to convince families to host a colle-giate soccer player for one week. This year a mom told me, "I was fearful of bringing someone we didn't know into our home, but when the week was over I cried because he was leaving. Next year, you can sign me up for a houseful."

As Christians, we believe all we've been given is for sharing, especially with the family of God. If you're like us, the timing will never be right. You won't have the extra money or beds or energy you'd like to have. You've read so many awful things, it seems like the best thing is to lock your doors tight and not let any strangers in.

Based on our journey these past few years, my words of advice are these: Don't wait for the Lord to break down your door. The hospitality you offer to a stranger will be a blessing, but the gifts back to your son and your family will be immeasurable.

34

A Son Needs His Mom to

Teach Him to Shine in the Dark

*Let your light shine before others, so that they may see your
good works and give glory to your Father who is in heaven.*

Matthew 5:16

About twenty minutes ago, my son Grayson came bursting through
the back door after school. "Mom!" he hollered to me.

"I'm in here, honey," I yelled back from my writing chair. "How was
school?"

Around the corner he came, and with no earthly idea what I'd been
doing all day, he just said this to me: "School was okay, but Mom, you
gotta know, it is so hard to be the light at that school. I mean it. Every
single day, I am completely surrounded by darkness. There is no way I
will ever be enough light."

"Grayson, do you know what I've been sitting here doing?"

"No."

"I've been writing about our call to be God's light in the darkness."

"No way."

"Way."

Grayson went on to tell me that he's not personally discouraged about
being just one of a few Jesus lights at his school. His frustration is that no
one seems to get it. The other students see his light. They respect his light.
They have even given him two nicknames—*Jesus* and *Sunshine* (I told him
I'd take either of those). But Grayson doesn't see anything changing. He
consistently shows up everyday bringing the light of Christ and the darkness never seems to budge.

Grayson intentionally chose a high school where he could lead the most kids to Christ. By the end of tenth grade, he was spiritually ready to be there and I never had a moment of hesitation about his decision. But I did think his mission was bigger than he could possibly have known at the time.

After his junior year and his shining fatigue, we asked if he'd like to transfer to another school to finish his senior year. He thought for just a minute and said, "I'd love to transfer next year. I know a lot of people at the other school and some of the teachers. It would be awesome to be at the same school with my brother and sister. But I just don't think that's what I'm supposed to do. As hard as it is some days, I feel liked I'm called to the school I'm attending."

That afternoon in my study, I tried to encourage his weary heart. I told him something like this:

"We are called to be obedient. We shine on assignment from God. Grayson, until graduation day, you have been divinely assigned to that school, those teachers, and the thousands of students who go there. Your only responsibility is to reflect back to them what God has done for you. You do that with your voice. The words you choose. Your work ethic. Your smile. Your servant's heart. Your compassion and your grace. Baby, you just get yourself over there every morning and shine bright as the sun.

"God has sent the Holy Spirit to take care of the change. You are planting seeds in the hearts of young men and women. You are radically and gently speaking the truths of Scripture, bold to say why you act the way you do and who is the Lord of your life. That is your assignment. The Holy Spirit will take care of the rest. You cannot put the whole school in a holy headlock until they cry, 'Jesus!'

"You may never know how many people will one day remember your light and the name Jesus and finally let the God of heaven set them free. But that's not your assignment. You're supposed to shine into their darkness. God loves them even more than you do and He will keep coming with His radiant light for all who have eyes to see."

As moms, we pray our boys will one day be ready to take the light of Christ into this dark world, not to be relegated to some corner, standing all alone, holding a tiny little flicker, but going into the darkness with the light inside of them burning brightly for all the world to see. Jesus said our assignment looks like this:

> You are the light of the world. A town built on a hill cannot be hidden. Neither do people light a lamp and put it under a bowl. Instead they put it on its stand, and it gives light to everyone in the house. In the same way, let your light shine before others, that they may see your good deeds and glorify your Father in heaven (Matthew 5:14-16).

Will you be intentional from the day your son is born to...

- pray he invites the light of Christ to burn brightly inside him.
- pray he falls passionately in love with his Savior.
- speak to him about this world using courageous and compassionate words.
- teach him that Jesus is our hope so we do not have to live in fear.
- remind him he is not alone. He belongs to your family. He belongs to the family of God.
- teach him the ways of God. Even in the dark, God is there. God works in the unseen. Behind the scenes. Deep in the hidden places of the heart.
- explain to him that when God sends a believer into the dark, He is at work.

Teaching our sons to shine in the dark will surely require more wisdom than you or I have. In order to give them what we have been given, we must remember this principle. The light of Christ in us increases with the nearness of God. We must stay with Jesus. Stay with Jesus.

May God glorify Himself in us. Let Him shine, baby. Let Him shine.

35

A Son Needs His Mom to

Take Him on a Ten Trip

*This is the day that the Lord has made;
let us rejoice and be glad in it.*

Psalm 118:24

The idea came to me when my oldest daughter, Taylor, was nine years old. I'd heard about a friend of a friend taking each one of her children on a special trip around the age of ten. Taylor was going to be ten and that mom's idea sounded like something we should do.

The only way to make this thing fly was to pitch the idea to all of the children as "The Ten Trip." *Taylor gets to go first because she'll be ten first, but each of you will get your turn.* They all went for it and gave the appearance of happiness when Taylor and I left for her Ten Trip to Chicago.

Four years later, Grayson turned ten. By then I was a single mom living as financially lean as I had ever known. I hoped they'd forget. Vocabulary words, they forget. Where they left their backpack, they forget. But the Ten Trip? In all those four years, no one ever forgot that promise.

Grayson really wanted to go to California for his Ten Trip, so this mom had some figuring out to do. Meanwhile, his scheming little brother, William, quietly pitched a plan to Grayson: "If you'll take me on your ten trip, I'll take you on mine. Let's go tell Mom we've made a deal." When they came in one night to tell me about their deal, the whole thing was pretty adorable. I didn't say yes, but I didn't say no, either.

Can you already hear the grace of God playing softly behind this story?

I'm not sure how I found coast-to-coast, round-trip plane tickets to Los Angeles for $200 each, but I did. I can't remember the name of the guy who gave us three tickets to the Lakers vs. Bulls basketball game, but I'm still grateful. I had some kind of a coupon for one-day passes to Disneyland, so we went. My dear friend Nicole invited us to sleep in her condo, so we stayed. My friends Dennis and Karen took us for In-and-Out Burgers and batting cages. By the time we flew home, Grayson's Ten Trip had become the most awesome adventure ever. To this day, I have never again flown round-trip to LAX for $200. And yes, those inexpensive flights sealed the deal for the sneaky stowaway. Grayson's Ten Trip (with William) went into the history books as some of their best days ever.

We were two Ten Trips down and still two to go.

William was probably four years old when I made the Ten Trip promise and I think that's also the day he chose New York City as his destination. At least I knew where we were going. After the miracle of Grayson's trip, I was determined to keep my promise to the others. With two years until the next trip, I began saving miles and points and dollars. Anything that might help us make it to the next one.

In my everyday life, I rarely ask anyone for anything. Really. I'll do almost anything to avoid asking for help. But with these Ten Trips, it's amazing what a mama will do. I have called in every favor I could think of for these trips. I've contacted strangers and told them our story. And the whole time, I've pretended to be braver than I'll ever really be. It's amazing what happens when a mom decides something must be done. She will rise up. Climb up. Stay up. Put up. You cannot mess with a mama on a mission!

Carried by grace and full of determination, this single mom pieced it all together again. William's Ten Trip (with Grayson) was another sweet miracle that included a Yankees baseball game, a high-rise room in a Times Square hotel, and the biggest ice cream sundae on the planet.

When I realized what these trips gave to each of my children, something in me kept trying to make them happen again. For each child, their Ten Trip was the most special thing to happen in their ten short years. None of them had ever been to their Ten Trip city and it was my complete joy and privilege to introduce them to another place in this world.

The lessons of traveling and exploring together were so much greater than I'd even hoped. After we had been in Chicago for a little less than a day, Taylor asked, "Mama, why do you keep giving money to people?" I realized the children had never been anywhere that tipping was expected. They didn't understand why I kept handing out a dollar here. Two dollars there. The cabbie. The doorman. The bellman. I loved telling them the tips were more than a gift. When they understood that's how those men make a living and feed their families, I'd catch them watching to make sure we'd given enough.

In New York, I wasn't sure if my boys would be interested in seeing a Broadway show, so I bought tickets to the Off Broadway production called Blue Man Group. They kept asking all kinds of questions that afternoon:

"What's it going to be like?"

"I'm not really sure, I've never seen it."

"How long do we have to sit in the theater?"

"About two hours, I think." I wondered if I'd made a mistake.

But from the first moment a blue man banged on a big drum, they were both riveted to the edge of their seats. The show whizzed by and before we knew it, we were standing in the lobby taking pictures with three men painted blue all over. Barely out the door of the theater, they begged me to see another show. There was no time that trip, but their appreciation for live production began that night. I loved being beside them for all of it.

I'm not sharing our Ten Trip stories with you so you'll feel some weird pressure to add one more thing to your life. But I do hope you're inspired to consider ways you'll introduce your son to things bigger than himself. Maybe your adventure will include travel. Maybe education or service or pets or nature or crafts or music or whatever your heart hears from God.

I also hope you heard these stories in a way that gives God the glory. I believe it was His grace that gave me the courage to dream about life-shaping adventures when the reality seemed so far away. His grace humbled me and taught me to ask for assistance.

Maybe you'll take your son on a Ten Trip one day. Or maybe your whole family will decide to adventure together down different roads with different goals. Whatever you do, I hope you dream up some big things, bigger than all of you, and then save and borrow and call in favors until you find a way to go do them together.

One last bit of information. Be prepared for the hucksters among you. What began as a promised ten-year-old trip for each child eventually became one trip for each child and three for William. When AnnaGrace's Ten Trip came around that child had sweet-talked himself onto another trip. The crazy thing is no one cares that he mooched their trip. The joy was multiplied when we were all together.

36

A Son Needs His Mom to

Make Christmas a Really Big Deal

*Be glad in the L*ORD*, and rejoice, O righteous, and*
shout for joy, all you upright in heart!

Psalm 32:11

It was September when the papers for my legal separation were drawn. By the following May, I was a divorced, single mom. All the days and months in between were without question the lowest of my entire life. Right in the middle of all that, there was Christmas. As I write this, my most vivid recollection is the pain. The pain…and also the shame.

The children and I lived in my parents' basement for four months. I was thankful to be with them for the holidays that year. I could barely feel myself breathe back then. I'm not sure how I could have put together a Christmas celebration. Mama and Daddy decorated the house and we did the regular "making cookies" kinds of things in an unsuccessful effort to hide the obvious. My four children and I were living out of suitcases, falling into the kindness of my family. They wanted us to be there. I was grateful, but I was numb. And it was Christmas.

That year was my first time our family "shared" Christmas Day. After I dropped the kids off with their father, it was an hour drive back to my parents' house. I have never cried with such a fury. I screamed until my voice was gone. It was the worst day of my life.

Mercifully, December became January. The kids were back and school began. After a couple of days, Grayson's teacher called me aside.

She said, "Angela, Grayson told me you didn't celebrate Christmas this year."

I died.

Before I could respond, the teacher continued, "I understand what you are going through right now. My daughter has gone through exactly the same thing. But I just want to encourage you about something. I know you are hurting, but these children are going to need you to set your pain aside and be their mom. You don't have to do everything, but you can try to do some things."

Her words to me were delivered with grace and concern. She was right and I had needed her tender rebuke. Who in the world knows how a woman with four children is supposed to behave while she's living with her parents and waiting for a divorce? I certainly didn't know how to act or what to do. Hiding with my shame, focused on my pain, it all seemed reasonable at the time.

At least a dozen years have passed since then. How appropriate that I can still see myself in her classroom that afternoon. The mom who for a moment became the student. My knees shoved underneath an elementary desk. My weary heart receiving her comfort with tears. The memory is vivid because the wisdom of her words guides me still.

Our sons need their mom to make Christmas a really big deal. And Easter. And Thanksgiving. And birthdays. And all the celebrations in between.

We are the memory makers. Moms make the traditions and set the tone. We must teach our sons how to celebrate so their hearts do not become fertile ground where Scrooge seeds can grow. As far as I can tell, these days there are too many family celebrations left undone. Too many neglected reasons for joy. Too many special moments left unnoticed. I let my whole family miss one Christmas, but by the grace of God and a wise schoolteacher, I decided that as far as I was able, my family would never spend a holiday or birthday like that again.

Here's what I wish I didn't need to clarify. When I say, "Make a really big deal out of Christmas," some are inclined to read, "Spend a lot of money." Too many are thinking, "It costs too much." Let's just settle this one right now. In my seven years as a single mom, I learned that celebration is more than anything an attitude of the heart. I did not have any extra money to spend. Ever. I learned to let my heart make joy anyway.

I'm not sure the children ever noticed or cared. The extra joy in the room cost little to nothing.

Around our house, "making a big deal" out of Christmas or any special day means…

Decorating with whatever we have or can make.

Inviting people over for potluck. If we all bring a little, we'll all be fed.

Music for any and every reason. *William, go put on the music you think goes with pizza!*

Handmade gifts. Notes. Art. I'm so grateful that handmade everything is cool again.

Conversations where people all cram into the same room. No TV allowed. Then they share one thing they like about the birthday boy. One favorite memory of Christmas. One thing they're grateful for at Thanksgiving. Like most new things you begin, you can count on awkward the first year, and the next year, not as much. Eventually, you'll get a tradition.

Games that include everyone. Every year, my husband, Scott, comes up with his Annual Thanksgiving Trivia Questions. He makes a big deal about how hard it's going to be for months. The family divides into pairs so no one has to look dumb all alone. There's usually a Disney movie question in there somewhere. A few sports questions. And the rest are up for grabs for those with the best grade school memories. The winner takes bragging rights. The losers complain about how many correct answers they erased. One tip: If you're ever at our house for Thanksgiving, make sure you get Uncle Walter as your partner.

There is a good chance you're a lot like me and by the time holidays roll around, your heart might be willing, but the rest of you is exhausted. There will be years to celebrate with less hoopla. Times to delegate a job to one of the children, knowing in advance it may not look exactly how you've always done it.

What I'm hoping is that you'll never be so paralyzed with pain or focused only on yourself that you do what I did. If it is in your power, do not miss one of those precious holidays you've been given with your family. Lead them with your heart full of celebration. May our sons become those rare kind of men who are able to celebrate with joy over all we have been given.

37

A Son Needs His Mom to

Take Him to Funerals and Visitations

For as in Adam all die, so also in Christ shall all be made alive.

1 Corinthians 15:22

Maybe it was just our family. Or maybe it was the size of our small community or church. But as far back as I can remember, there were many times my parents would call me and my brothers inside, clean us up, change our clothes, and put us all in the car to "run by the funeral home." Someone I probably didn't know very well had died, and my parents wanted to pay their respects. That meant we all went to the funeral home together.

I don't think my parents ever considered not taking us with them or dropping us off with a babysitter. We'd probably see other kids we knew and spend half the night trying to run when we were supposed to be quiet and begging for quarters for the snack machines around back. Our whole town responded to death the same way. Families came en masse to support one another with their presence and lots of food.

Since being a mom, I haven't lived in the same kind of close-knit community I grew up in. I'm sure people in my town have died at about the same rate as before, but I haven't known many of them. "Running by the funeral home," isn't something my children have done nearly as often.

One of the first times I planned to take my children to a visitation, a friend called and asked if they were going. I told her it hadn't occurred to me not to take them. She said she didn't think her similar-aged son was ready to go to something like that. And based on the rest of our conversation, I'm sure he wasn't ready to go either. Their family had only discussed death and funerals in hushed whispers, allowing the imagery of Halloween caskets and gravestones to fill in the blanks of his imagination. Poor kid.

Everything my friend said that day affirmed my decision to take my kids to funerals as often as it was appropriate. The sooner they were exposed to these kinds of events, the sooner I'd have the opportunity to speak God's peace into their fears.

I heard the story of a little boy who became terrified walking into the room for his grandfather's visitation. His terror became screaming and near panic. His parents couldn't understand his extreme reaction and took him outside for a talk. On the lawn of the funeral home, the reason for his hysterics became clear. The boy told his parents he didn't want to see his grandfather without his head. Bless his soul. He'd heard the adults talking about "taking the body" to the funeral home and his literal mind assumed the body would be present but the head would not.

Can I encourage you to begin taking your son to visitations and funerals as early as possible? Speak to him with words that convey your own grief and sadness. Be sensitive to his fears. There is no need to force him to view the casket if he's not ready. Don't use easily misunderstood phrases to describe death. *Great-grandpa is sleeping. We lost our neighbor today.* Make sure he can feel the reassurance of your comfort. Be honest about the circumstances of death, reserving any details that might be age-inappropriate. Make sure he is part of the celebration, hearing loved ones share their good memories and telling the funny stories that still bring laughter.

And use this moment to teach him again about our Savior, Jesus, who died on the cross, but three days later rose from the dead, promising all who believe the same victory over death and eternal life with Him.

Almost two years ago, my mama went to heaven. And it was just like everyone says: Even though she'd been sick, none of us were ready to let her go. Thankfully, God allowed our family the time to purposefully gather around her in the last hours of her life. My boys came straight to the hospital from a soccer tournament. Still in their uniforms, they rushed home when the doctor said it was time. They'd been to see their grandmother in the hospital many times, but this time was different and we all knew it. Mama was able to acknowledge their arrival. They hugged her and kissed her and I watched their hearts break from across the room.

When the whole family filled her room, we talked to her just like we were all standing in the kitchen. Making little jokes we hoped would make her smile, then deciding she might like to hear us all sing. With the words to some of her favorite hymns on our iPhones, my brother led our little family choir through the verses. Eventually, Daddy told us all to go home and a couple of hours later, Mama stepped from death into glory.

Our boys need their mom to teach them what death and funerals mean on earth and the joy of what they mean in heaven.

This poem might do that as beautifully as anything I've ever read.

> I am standing upon the seashore. A ship at my side spreads her white sails to the moving breeze, and starts for the blue ocean. She is an object of beauty and strength, and I stand and watch her until she hangs like a speck of white cloud just where the sea and sky come down to meet and mingle with each other. Then someone at my side says: "There! She's gone!" Gone where? Gone from my sight—that is all. She is just as large in mast and hull and spar as she was when she left my side, and just as able to bear her load of living freight to the place of her destination. Her diminished size is in me, and not in her.

> And just at that moment when someone at my side says: "There! She's gone!" there are other eyes that are watching for her coming; and other voices ready to take up the glad shout: "There she comes!"

> And that is—"dying."*

---

* Luther F. Beecher, "What Is Dying?" *Northwestern Christian Advocate,* July 13, 1904, 14.

38

A Son Needs His Mom to

Order Him into the Creek

As for the rich in this present age, charge them not to be haughty, nor to set their hopes on the uncertainty of riches, but on God, who richly provides us with everything to enjoy.

1 Timothy 6:17

Several years ago, a group of my church friends decided we'd bring our kids and meet for a hike in the mountains. Altogether, I bet there were 25 or 30 of us. The moms were happy to be together that spring morning and the kids were chatty and silly and fun. Arriving at the trail, we discovered a beautiful, unhurried mountain stream would match every twist and turn of our trek. The day was warm, but we walked underneath a canopy of trees, cooled by a breeze that felt like perfection. I can still see all those kids without a care in the world, perched around on big rocks, munching their backpack lunches. The moms still talk about the time we took a perfect hike on a perfect day.

Near the end of our return, we came to a place where the stream beside us spread wide. The water was shallow and moving with ease. We all looked at one another and quickly voted for a moment of spontaneity. "Let's get in the creek," we all told our children. No one had planned for this. We didn't have a towel among us. We just decided the creek would be fun and we'd drive home a little wet and the joy was more important than dry clothes. We even said, "Leave your shoes on so you won't slip." You've never seen a pile of kids get in a creek any faster. They were elated to get in the water—especially with all their clothes on!

I'd been helping my children find their way over the rocks when I glanced up to see Grayson backing away. One of my friends took the hands of my children and I went over to my firstborn son. I guess he was somewhere around six years old.

"Hey, honey, let's get in the creek," I said, taking his cute little hands in mind.

"I don't want to."

"What do you mean, you don't want to? The water is warm. It won't even be as high as your knees. The stream is moving really slowly, so there's nothing to be afraid of. We'll all be together. I will hold on to you. Look at William and AnnaGrace—they're laughing and having a great time."

"I don't want to. We didn't bring a towel and I don't want to get wet."

"It doesn't matter, baby. No one has a towel so we'll all be wet. It's okay. We'll all ride home wet together. It'll be fun."

"I don't want to," was his adamant, blue-eyed resolve.

Not really sure what to do with this unexpected quandary, I walked back into the water and left Grayson on a rock a few feet from the creek. He looked like he wanted to cry, sitting there watching his friends laugh and splash and play. I felt like I wanted to cry. My lighthearted, skipping boy had been stopped in his tracks.

Standing in that perfect mountain holler stream on that perfect blue-sky day, I had an immediate flashback. I was sitting on my hundredth amusement park bench while everyone else rode the roller coaster behind me. My fears never allowed me to ride anything past the kiddie park. Junior high. High school. College. Student ministry leader. I sat out every ride for all of those years. When I looked back at Grayson, I glimpsed the me he could become.

Out of the water and back to the rock that held Grayson, I knelt in front of him so he could see my compassion. I explained what I had just remembered. I told him my heart was full of love for him and that love was the reason for what I said next: "Grayson, as your mom, I am ordering you to get into the creek. If you get into the creek up to your knees and you don't like being there, I'll get you out. But I will not let you decide from the bank."

He looked at me like I'd just told him to jump from a plane. I was kind but unmoved. His eyes filled with tears and it broke my heart, but I said, "Grayson, you don't have a say in this. I am ordering you to go stand in that creek."

It's still awful remembering how afraid he was and how stern I had to be in that moment. All those other kids were there and his mom had given him no options, so with tears in his eyes, Grayson obediently marched slowly down into the creek. I fully expected him to be carrying him back to dry land in less than 30 seconds. But right then and there, a full-fledged miracle occurred. All his friends were happy to see him, so Grayson stood still while they began to slog and splash to come to him. In just a few seconds, I watched one of his hands reach down to feel the stream move between his fingers. Then the next hand. And before I knew what happened, Grayson took a big swing and splashed water on the friend who had finally gotten to him. The friend laughed and splashed back. Grayson laughed and splashed harder, all his tears washed away.

We were a hardworking family growing up, and play didn't have much value in our house. It was an unspoken principle we assumed everybody else knew: People who played games and went on rides at the amusement park wasted precious time that could have been spent working. My family jokingly said of my grandfather, "Papa quit school because they had recess. He didn't like to play." To this day, I am still trying to overcome the recess-avoidant genes I was given.

That day by the creek was a big one for me. Ordering Grayson into the water was something of a personal declaration: Hiking trails that wind through the mountains are God's creation. Flowing streams sing the music He composed. A blue-sky day is His original masterpiece. God gives these gifts for us to enjoy.

When we receive His goodness with open hands and enjoy His glory with open hearts, that joy will many days look exactly like play. Don't forget to teach your son how to play.

39

A Son Needs His Mom to
Remain Steady When He Doubts

You will seek me and find me, when you seek me with all your heart.

Jeremiah 29:13

God, in His wisdom, entrusted me with two boys who are nothing if not thinkers. Many days I'm unsure I'm the best one for the job, but I guess it doesn't matter now. They are mine. I'm honored to be the mom of boys who challenge me intellectually to hang on for all I'm worth.

As little boys, they both seemed to be the regular kind of curious, sometimes asking questions, but mostly trusting what they were taught in school or church. Now as teenagers, they are becoming very scholarly men with layers of curiosity and lots of questions. At least for now, their core interests include philosophy, theology, art, and science, with a smattering of French along the way. One leans more philosophical, the other more scientific. Both of them can make my head hurt in under five minutes.

Here's the thing. I'm crazy about my thinker-boys. But when you are a thinker, there is the nagging desire to get "it" all figured out. When "it" is a chemistry experiment or French verb test, getting it all figured out is awesome. When "it" is teaching yourself how to edit videos or play the piano, figuring it out is double awesome. But when "it" is God, then mercy. Lord, have mercy.

Both of our sons chose to become followers of Jesus sometime after kindergarten, but the deeper questions and discussions about God seemed to begin around 14. In the past few years, those minds have kicked into high gear, processing ideologies and principles at least ten years ahead of where I was at their age. Then one day, Grayson finally said it out loud:

"Mom, I'm really struggling with my doubts about God." I leaned across the kitchen counter and asked, "What kind of questions are you having?" I think we've been having one big ongoing discussion ever since.

I'll save you the details of earth-age theories, the worldview matrix, and apologetic debates, because there's no reason to make your head hurt too. Besides, our sons do not need us to have all the answers for every spiritual question they will face. What they do need is a mom who is not afraid of doubt. They need a mom who is secure in her own faith and wise enough to understand that great men of God will journey through seasons of doubt in order to know Him more.

From my own years of searching, studying, and questioning, here's what I have discovered: I do not have to be afraid of my son's spiritual doubts or questions. If my boys are seeking answers for gigantic theological issues or struggling openly with their doubts, I will do everything I can to help. But more importantly, I have learned I can trust God to deliver His answers. His way. In His time.

God is not diminished by our questions.

God is not weakened by our doubt.

God does not withhold His love from those who struggle to resolve the tensions among science, philosophy, and faith.

As a matter of fact, God said, "You will seek me and find me when you seek me with all your heart" (Jeremiah 29:13).

We've already had more conversations than I can count and I'm sure there will still be more. No matter how we begin, I usually end up saying something like this.

"Honey, I'm not afraid of your questions or doubts. I'm not alarmed or troubled because I did the same thing. I was much older than you when I finally had more questions about God than I had answers, but here is what I found: If you will seek God for His answers and His peace, you will find them. Really. Truly. He may not work on your timeframe or shout audibly to you from a megaphone, but I am absolutely sure that the one who seeks God will find Him.

"When I think about your intellectual struggle to know God, I have to believe a strong foundation is being built in your soul. A great man does not casually accept the ideas or traditions of others as his own. A great man becomes wise because he works to acquire and understand knowledge. Truth is valuable to him and he will not settle for secondhand reasoning. Nothing of value comes without effort. The wisdom you gain on this journey will become like treasure for your life.

"So I want you to seek God with every question and every doubt. I don't have any faith in my ability to answer your questions. I am absolutely assured of His.

"The work of searching for the answers of God builds a solid foundation in your soul. A foundation that will not be shaken. A foundation you can build your life on. Others may settle for the answers that come from clichés or headlines, but not you. You will have God's answers. And your soul will be at peace."

My sister-in-law told me this story the other day. Her son, Holden, had written a senior essay for his college application. Like any good mother, she had gone behind him to see what he'd written. The part that took her breath away was the paragraph he wrote about deciding to follow Jesus. Holden had written, "My mom has always taken us to church, so I've heard a lot about God in my life. But by age 15, I had pretty much decided I didn't believe in Him.

"One night I was thinking about the whole faith thing and had an idea I thought would finally settle the issue once and for all. I said to God, 'If You are real, then show me.'

"The next few weeks all I could see was God. Everywhere I looked, there was something God was doing. Some new evidence of His presence or His power. I gave my life to Him because I was so overwhelmed by His answer to my doubting prayer."

I cried like a baby when Holden decided to follow Jesus. Happy for him and grateful for our God who doesn't hold grudges against doubters.

Moms can remain steady when our sons wrestle with doubt because we know the One who is faithful.

40

A Son Needs His Mom to
Buy Him a Rubik's Cube

*For everything there is a season, and a time
for every matter under heaven.*

Ecclesiastes 3:1

Now that our children are older, Christmas gifts could easily become the time I get caught up on their practical needs. This one needs jeans, that one, new boots. A few years ago, I had been shopping a little here and a little there. Then one morning I couldn't remember what I'd hidden in the secret place. So into the crumpled bags I went. By the time I sorted and stacked six neat little piles all around me, I felt like I'd turned into Scrooge. There before me sat six, pitiful heaps of practicality. There wasn't one fun toy or puzzle or anything like those Christmas mornings filled with Rescue Heroes and Legos.

Right then and there I decided I had to save Christmas! I decided as long as I'm in charge of Santa's workshop, there will always be a little something fun or frivolous for each one.

Hence, the decision to buy a Rubik's Cube for William's stocking.

Please note: I did not say the fun and frivolous little gifts I bought for my teenage boys sent their hearts a flutter and their feet a dancin'. This mom is going to keep bringing the fun. Whether they choose to hoot and holler like old times is their teenage boy choice.

Anyway, back to the cube.

William was in the ninth grade that Christmas. Sometime in the afternoon, he neatly stacked his practical gifts with the boxed cube on top and took his Christmas plunder up to his room. And that was the end of that.

The stocking stuffer I chose especially for the son who might enjoy the challenge sat on his desk in its box until June.

Like the toys in the *Toy Story* movie, it probably spun around on its corner and laughed every time I left his room.

But June came, school was out, and one slow, summer day, William came into the kitchen with his Christmas cube. If I had to guess, I'd say he was bored out of his mind, unboxed the cube, got frustrated that solving wasn't as easy as he'd assumed, then came downstairs to Google ways to beat the cube.

William can explain from here. I lifted the following paragraphs from one of his senior essays.

> Three years ago, I received a Rubik's Cube for Christmas but never played with it. I reckoned the 3D game a better paperweight than brain puzzle. But eventually, curiosity overcame my low opinion. An event that left me, hysterically, attempting to rearrange those colors. I couldn't solve the cube, but I was sure someone, somewhere, had to know how.
>
> The Internet led to my cubing enlightenment. As it turns out, one solves a 3x3 cube, or any size cube, via a series of algorithms. Once the solver observes the current "situation" of the cube, he applies the corresponding algorithm and the cube has no other choice but to react to the taming twists and turns thusly. My cubing liberation came from a diligence not to throw in the towel, or rather, cube.
>
> A six-sided cube taught me I can learn anything if I put my mind to it. It felt powerful to use my mind to solve something hard.

Here's where I must warn you. If low-level clicking sounds get on your nerves, then do not buy your son a Rubik's Cube. When a boy decides to attempt the cube challenge, he will become quiet, but the constant clicking of plastic tiles accompanied by swooshes of quickly turning rows will become louder and louder. The summer of William's infatuation, our family took several flights together. As God would have it, William's seat was behind mine for over 24 hours of flying. I almost. Lost. My. Mind.*

Here's the crazy thing, I had no idea solving a Rubik's Cube was all about math. For the love. Observing the cube and memorizing algorithms? Are you kidding me? But that's not all! After a player "tames" the six sides, only a spark of addictive fire has been lit. The next level is speed. Timing yourself. Beating your time. And then there's competition. Competing with fellow cube-tamers for the fastest times. At this writing, the world record for cube solving is 7.3 seconds. Yep. I said seconds. There's a video. And a competition in Vegas. It's a crazy cube world out there. As William said, "It was fun to watch my cubing infatuation become like fire."

By the end of summer, we had a full-on blaze. William had worked his cube skills at soccer practice and the soccer boys began buying their own cubes. School began in the fall and the frenzy was unleashed. Algorithm tutoring was in high demand, so William hand-wrote a "Rubik's Cube Solving Manual" and made copies to distribute. By second semester, the headmaster was forced to address the school-wide Rubik's Cube distraction, directing the students to keep all cubes in their backpacks during classroom instruction. I am not kidding.

I'll let William continue from his essay:

> It's been three years and I keep a check on our school's cubing pulse. Like myself, there are still those who can't put down the "six sides." The cubing phenomenon at my school makes me chuckle. It's cool to see what curiosity and diligence can do.

To this day I believe the cube unlocked something in William's mind. Training his mind to arrange the colors was fun, but even better was tutoring his friends and watching them enjoy the same challenge.

So buy your son a Rubik's Cube. Be sure to call it a game—and I don't think there's any need to mention all that algorithm stuff. Watch that box

---

* As we journeyed further into cube-land, we discovered a cube lube oil, which produces slicker, faster, and mercifully, quieter cube solving. No doubt, the invention of a near-bonkers mom.

sit on his desk for six months to a year. You can "just happen" to show him some competition videos.

Maybe he'll get bored one day and reach for the cube. Better than a video game. Requiring no batteries, electricity, or Internet connection, the cube just might unlock something for your son too.

May the algorithm fires ignite in your home!

41

A Son Needs His Mom to
Send Him Out for Adventure and Pray Him Home for Love

Above all, keep loving one another earnestly.

1 Peter 4:8

Our 20-year-old son, Grayson, will be landing at the airport near our house in about two hours. He's been in Brazil for the past 62 days and just boarded the last of his three flights home.

Every mom I know would have slept exactly the way I slept last night. My head was propped on a couple of pillows facing the nightstand beside my bed. On top of the table, there was a stack of books high enough to hold my computer about eye level. Then I left my computer open and running all night so I could track Grayson's flight coming home. Eventually my waking and sleeping found a rhythm.

I must have fallen asleep.

A groggy click to refresh the browser. Held breath.

Why is this computer so slow?

A blinking icon appears on a black screen. I exhale deep.

Hey, honey, there you are. I hope you're sleeping.

Thank You, Jesus. Lord, please keep bringing my boy home.

Every hour or so, I'd wake enough to watch a tiny computer-generated airplane, with exactly the right flight numbers, slowly work its way north across the map of South America. When your son has been gone too long and too far and now he's at 40,000 feet for most of the night, a blinking light on a computer screen is like the Lord Himself speaking, *I have your boy. He is safe and here is a blinking light to quiet your mama's heart. Trust Me. You can go back to sleep.*

When Grayson first called to talk about the possibility of going to Brazil, I asked some really good questions and listened to his enthusiastic answers. As the conversation progressed, we talked through the big ideas of who and where and why. Grayson had a lot of passion about the trip, but honestly, not many details. Moms who are considering their son spending a summer in a foreign country just want a few basic facts. Things like,

What is the city in Brazil?

Where would you stay?

What will you be doing?

How will you eat?

How much will it cost?

Honey, what exactly is the name of the mission organization?

By the end of our first conversation, I realized Grayson didn't have the answers to any of those questions. The most important thing to Grayson was whether or not God wanted him to go. Details were not really on his radar yet because his passion was engaged and he knew he was supposed to go.

Now, this is just about the time I would have previously shut this whole thing down. I could have easily thrown down the logic card: "If you don't even know where this trip is going or what you will be doing or who in the world is in charge of this thing, I'd say you're probably not supposed to be there." Or the fear of crime card: "I don't think you need to be anywhere near the World Cup for your first solo trip to a foreign country." So I kept waiting for my heart to object. My head already had a hundred reasons this was the dumbest idea ever, but something in my heart would not budge. In my spirit, I did not have any indication God was prompting me to say no.

So I said the craziest thing ever. "Grayson, I think you're supposed to go."

It was a long spring of me begging for more details and helping him sort this thing out. Grayson made two trips to Washington to get his visa. (He had to go a second time because he got to the Brazilian consulate and didn't have the correct identification.) He raised his support to pay for lodging and food we hoped would appear. I booked his round-trip flights but they were the wrong dates. I rebooked his flights and paid the big fee.

Two days before Grayson was supposed to leave, his passport and visa had not arrived. We checked everything known to humankind. The post office said they had delivered it a week ago. We tore our house apart and finally spread tarps on the driveway to sort through a week's trash.

You guessed it. No United States passport. No Brazilian visa.

About seven o'clock that night, I called the State Department. A nice man sympathized with our predicament and offered this: "Ma'am, the only option you have is to be in Washington, D.C. tomorrow morning at seven thirty. If you're lucky, your son might have a passport and new visa before the day ends. But I can't promise anything."

That was the exact moment I began to doubt. Maybe I had been wrong. Maybe Grayson wasn't supposed to go to Brazil this summer. We were 36 hours away from takeoff and this great idea of a mission trip was feeling more like a really bad dream. The whole thing had been too hard and now, by no fault of his own, at the eleventh hour, all Grayson's travel documents were lost.

What happened next is still a shock to me. I hung up the phone, looked at Grayson, and said, "Pack your toothbrush. We're driving to Washington."

"Right now?"

"Yep, right now. You're driving. I'll find a room on the way. I think we can make it by two o'clock, sleep for a few hours, and be first in line at the Passport Agency tomorrow morning."

He grinned.

I said, "We have to try. If we do all this and don't get the documents, we'll deal with that later. But tonight, we have to try."

In case you haven't driven into our nation's capital at two o'clock in the morning, you should know it's a stunning sight. Past the Jefferson Memorial and around the Lincoln, I was grateful I got to see the city like that…one time.

The next day was a bona fide miracle. From the Passport Agency we ran to the Brazilian consulate, then back and forth three more times. At

11:45 a.m., we walked out of the Brazilian consulate with tears in our eyes. We had in our hands a brand new United States passport and a reissued, without charge, Brazilian visa. The kindness given to us that day was so lavish, we almost, for a second, felt guilty.

Adventures begin for our boys before they can walk, and then, by the grace of God, they get to spend a lifetime looking for the next escapade. The first time your baby boy dismounts the crib and sticks the landing, it's on. Over a lifetime, I estimate we'll tell them "No!" at least a billion times.

But one day, that son of yours will come running in the back door devising his next adventure. You'll listen to the grand plan of it all, preparing the way you're going to say, "Not yet" once again. But that day, the Holy Spirit won't let you speak. You'll be like an old lady frantically checking her pockets for the key she always has. *My no has to be around here somewhere. I've never misplaced it before.*

Not misplaced. Only removed.

The Holy Spirit will nudge your heart, *He's ready. I'll take care of him. Today is the day you say yes.*

When the Holy Spirit says yes, send that son of yours out for adventure. Then prop your head on a pillow, squint over at a screen all hours of the night, and pray him home safely with your love.

42

A Son Needs His Mom to

Stop Yelling

Out of the abundance of the heart the mouth speaks.

Luke 6:45

I totally get it. I have done it myself. I have heard plenty of others. And I believe I understand why moms yell at their kids. Moms yell because yelling is easy.

There you go. Pretty deep psychology, huh? The truth is, it's just easier to yell. It requires no movement on your part. You can scream from the kitchen. Shout from the laundry room. Holler and carry on while still safely buckled into the driver's seat of your car. It's easy.

And it's lazy.

And it's scary.

And I hate the way screaming makes your throat feel.

So one day, I stopped. Just went cold turkey. No seminars. No coaching. No manual on what to use instead of volume. I decided to stop yelling at my kids and that was it. Forever. My hope is that you will decide to stop yelling too.

I realize some of you grew up in a home where people yelled at one another. It's all you've ever known. It feels natural to you, and there is a possibility you don't even realize when you do it. Yelling doesn't even hurt because those muscles in your throat are tough as leather from all their use.

I didn't grow up in a yelling house. But I picked it up easily enough. Actually, when I think about it, yelling at my child wasn't something I intentionally "picked up" and started doing. It's the kind of thing you don't even know you can do until you've furrowed your brow, narrowed your eyes, and then heard crazy-woman screeching come from your very own mouth.

When a mom is totally exhausted and exasperated, you'd think all she'd be able to do is whisper. But oddly enough, those are exactly the times when a simple instruction for a disobedient toddler is able to come from you with a fierce volume and power you've never known.

May I give you a few reasons to stop yelling at your son today?

1. You are smarter than that.

2. You are more creative than that.

3. You are scary and a scary mom is never a good thing. They make horror movies about moms like that.

4. Yelling may result in momentary obedience, but you are not the army and he is not a soldier. There will not be any long-term gain for either of you.

5. A firm voice with grace-filled instruction is the evidence of a secure mom.

6. Taking the easy, lazy way today will, over time, become a habit for you both. You will become that obnoxious mom and he will become that obnoxious kid.

7. You are teaching him to yell like you do.

8. There is this thing called childhood memory. I am certainly no psychologist, but from some of my adult friends, I have learned that being yelled at as a child is a memory with great power. Maybe even enough power to overshadow what was good. When that happens, those kids grow up and say things like, *I seem to remember lots of yelling.*

Before I leave you with the wrong impression, I never really yelled at my children very much. When I was tired. Or when they were tired. Or both. I was an occasional screamer. But I still hated every occasional time I did.

The day I stopped yelling forever, I had barked an exasperated order and then one more time for good measure, except louder. Thankfully, I can't remember which child was standing in front of me. All I remember was the look of hurt in his eyes. A hurt I'd never meant to give. The kind of hurt could easily become anger one day. And I was done.

Deciding not to bark orders at my children meant I had to change a few things.

Instead of yelling, "Don't touch that!" for the tenth time, I had to consistently get up and go to my child to discipline him in person instead of from across the room.

I had to teach my children to obey my sweet words instead of waiting for my screeching words. The sweet words weren't coming anymore, so I had to spend some time undoing my poor parenting technique.

I found that I learned so much more about each of the children by using a firm voice, being up close, and looking into their eyes. My nearness was about relationship even when I had walked over to them to redirect or discipline. A steady voice from me, no matter how they'd behaved, began to communicate a security to them. We were building our relationship instead of building walls I'd have to try to tear down one day.

The Bible says that from the mouth comes the overflow of the heart. In order to keep my commitment, I had to fill my heart with wisdom and grace. I wanted to speak to my children from that overflow.

There have been some moments, especially as the boys got older, when all I could think to do in a situation was yell. My head couldn't come up with anything better at the time. In those moments, I have chosen to leave the room. Or stop the car. Or whatever I had to do to disconnect from my intense frustration or disappointment. Whatever emotion I could have released by yelling still wasn't worth it to me.

As a mom, I'm a soul shaper. Foundation builder. Character giver. That kind of mom gets creative about how to communicate with her son, or gets over it. That mom sets a righteous tone for her home. She speaks with wisdom. Fills with grace. May we grow in spiritual maturity, becoming moms who measure our words and weigh our motives. May we cherish this opportunity to raise our sons, determined to remove yelling and screaming from the lines in our story.

43

A Son Needs His Mom to

Make Home the Safest Place

*My people will abide in a peaceful habitation, in
secure dwellings, and in quiet resting places.*

Isaiah 32:18

My early years were spent in a small house in a small town. The ins and outs of our everyday life were by all standards ordinary. Regular. Average. We were just a normal family living a fairly typical American life. Hardworking. Churchgoing. And probably kind of boring. As far as I knew, everybody else was doing about the same as me.

And then I grew up.

As a grown woman, I now realize that my parents gave our family an uncommon gift. Every day we all came home to nothing fancy, but our regular, run-of-the-mill home was always the safest place on earth.

As a mom who is trying to pay attention, I have watched my kids' friends and listened to their comments. For a lot of them, home is a tough place to be. Growing up is hard enough. When a boy has a safe place to grow, it will become a gift to him. A character-shaping gift.

In a safe home, complete and total acceptance is a given. If you wake up with bedhead, it's okay, because you're home. If you have a big, red sty on your eye or acne all over your face, no one in your family is ashamed to be seen with you. They are with you for the long haul, pimples and all.

People in a safe home care where you're going, who you are with, and when you'll be home. They don't care because they distrust you. They care because they love you so.

Correction and discipline are given with grace. The punishment fits the crime.

Parents are not angry about childish mistakes. Children can be childish and clumsy and flat-out awkward. The dumbest, most inconvenient things happen in a family. There will be frustration but not misplaced emotion. Emotion is misplaced when people rage over a poorly cut lawn but feel nothing about the reports of hunger or trafficking in their town.

In a safe home, your mistakes and consequences are not held against you. Growing up means I may have done something dumb yesterday, but I am learning and today I am trying to do better than before. Safe families grieve your mistakes and your consequences, but they do not keep reminding you of the person you have been. They choose instead to believe in the person you can be.

The people in your family are always happy to see you.

A safe home is a soft place to fall. When you flat-out fail and fall on your face, home is the place that breaks your landing.

The pressure of the world falls away and you are reminded over and over that you are loved. You are accepted. You have nothing to prove to the people you love. You want to do your best because they support you.

There are no eggshells underneath your feet.

There are no questions about love. It does not have to be earned. Or proven. It cannot be bought. Or stolen. Or lost. Love is a given. A regular, everyday given.

No one wakes up and worries, *What will I do wrong today? What will they blame me for this time?*

You are not expected to act older when you are still young. You are not allowed to act younger when you're old enough.

Your family knows as long as you have one another, no matter what comes, you will be okay.

Jesus Christ is the center of the family. Not one parent or one child. Always, above all else, in all things, Jesus.

44

A Son Needs His Mom to

Tell Him a Real Man Doesn't Fear a Room Full of Estrogen

Do not judge by appearances, but judge with right judgment.

John 7:24

Before we begin, I'd like to make a personal declaration. There have been many times when I desired to be funny or bring a moment of levity to a situation. And then, in the effort to be quick on my feet, what my head had intended for humor, embarrassingly, came out of my mouth sounding like the dumbest thing ever.

Days after a moment of great dumb-ness, I'm usually still kicking myself mentally, *Angela, what in the world just happened? You are more compassionate than that. You're more educated than that. You're more self-less than that.*

So here's the deal, a person can have a really great heart and still, unintentionally, say something stupid. It's a proven fact.

But, there are at least two more reasons people say stupid things. Either they have not been taught, or stupid is the chosen condition of their heart.

Jesus said, "The good person out of the good treasure of his heart produces good, and the evil person out of his evil treasure produces evil, for out of the abundance of the heart his mouth speaks" (Luke 6:45).

Our sons, fully in their humanity, are going to make all kinds of mistakes. They will say dumb things they never meant. Make quick judgments without facts. Repeat what they heard someone else say, instead of forming their own opinions.

I do not write these next words to be a man-basher. My assignment for this book is much higher than that.

So here goes.

Almost 100 percent of my work means I will be communicating to a group of women. Small groups. Large groups. Doesn't matter. These groups of women are all over the place. East coast. West coast. Doesn't matter. Every so often, a man will be in the room. All kinds of men, pastors: janitors, sound guys, band guys, husbands, board members, movie stars. Doesn't matter.

And too many times, in too many ways, I've been in the room when one of those guys blurts out something stupid to that group of women...

Whoa, there sure is a lot of estrogen in this room. I gotta get out of here.

Is this where the hens are meeting? Thought I heard the cackling down the hall.

I'll just leave y'all to talk about your girly things now. Whatever that is.

Whew, this is too much estrogen for me. I need to go outside and bench press something.

I could keep going, but I'll spare you. With only a few phrases, I am certain you get my point.

Why in the world would a man, standing in a room full of women, blurt out such small-minded drivel? Maybe it was an honest, unintended, dumb thing. Maybe he just said what he's heard other men say. Maybe insecurity. Lack of training. Arrogance.

With a heart full of grace, I'd like to say a few things to some of those grown men:

Making fun of women will never make you more masculine.

You do not endear yourself to anyone when you insinuate that a real man wouldn't be caught dead at a meeting of primarily women.

Sometimes, when you're "just teasing," the truth in your heart comes through loud and clear. We hear more than you realize. Probably more than you meant for us to know.

There were wounded women in the room where you just "ran from the estrogen." You did not cause those wounds, nor does anyone hold you responsible for their healing. But for just a moment, you had the opportunity to demonstrate how a great man speaks to other women.

If a man came to marry your daughter, then you overheard him dismiss her opinions because of "hormones," he made fun of her hobbies, sewing or white-water rafting or whatever, then told her the higher register of her laughter sounded just like a hen. Well, I imagine you'd send that man packing.

My husband, Scott, has been selling trucks for 28 years. As a matter of fact, the trucks he sells are the largest trucks manufactured in North America. He is surrounded by manly-men all day long. Mechanics, drivers, engineers, and customers who need trucks for the toughest jobs, construction, concrete, drilling. Believe me when I say, my 6'4", Ironman-finishing, truck-selling husband is all man, all the time.

When we were just beginning to date, I kept trying to describe to Scott what I do. I speak at women's conferences all over the world. All women. All the time. Truck business. Women's ministry. I think we can all agree those two things lack a natural connection. I couldn't imagine how a man like Scott would survive in my world.

In the effort to scare him off early, I asked Scott to come to some women's events where I was speaking. I was sure "all that estrogen" would give him the willies and our dating would come to a grinding halt. I liked him a lot, but I didn't want this to drag on if my world was too "girly."

There are a million things I'd love to tell you about Scott, but for today, here is the one of the best things I have learned from him. A real man isn't afraid of a room full of estrogen. They don't feel the need to run outside and do pushups. Real men don't carelessly joke about women's tears or the squeal of their laughter. Real men esteem God's design and value all the ways we are different. Real men sit down with women and have conversations and get their jokes and protect their hearts. Real men keep trying to learn how to communicate value to other women, whether she is an employee, a casual acquaintance, his step-daughter, or his wife.

So mom-friend of mine, instead of man-bashers, let us become man-shapers. You and I have the privilege of teaching our sons how to communicate value to women wherever they are.

Explain gender differences to him all along the way. Always assign the same value to both. Remind him of the Creator's wisdom in the design.

When you hear an off-handed remark about a woman, remind your son that a great man would never say that.

Teach him that little words and little jokes can communicate big things. Use even the little words for good.

Teach him that strong men are able to use soft words.

A room full of women is a force that can change the world. Respecting those hearts is more powerful than diminishing them.

Real men are still real men even if they spend all weekend in an arena of 20,000 women.

Real men are still real men even if the speaker never uses one football illustration to make her point.

May our sons never feel the need to diminish a woman's beautiful design. Not for a laugh. Not from their insecurity. Not from ignorance.

Let's teach them well.

A Son Needs His Mom to

Teach Him About Christians, Jews, Muslims, Hindus, Atheists, and Kindness

But when the goodness and loving kindness of God our Savior appeared, he saved us, not because of works done by us in righteousness, but according to his own mercy, by the washing of regeneration and renewal of the Holy Spirit, whom he poured out on us richly through Jesus Christ our Savior.

Titus 3:4-6

Here is how the story was told to me:

It was our first day on the new team. I knew my son was a little anxious, so I decided to stick around and watch practice. I didn't want to embarrass him or have him accuse me of hovering, so I sat in a chair beside the field and pretended to read a book. Far enough away but close enough to hear.

I guess I stayed that day because of the weekend before.

The weekend before, my son attended an elementary birthday party with some kids from school. A few boys in his class learned we are Jewish. One comment led to another and they ended up cornering my son and taunting him. Among many things, they told him he was going to hell. There were some tears and hurtful words. The whole thing was more like a trial than a party. I was so sad for my son that day.

We had several family discussions the week between the party and the practice. My son has a strong spirit and a good understanding of his heritage. I know he's going to be fine. But, that day, the mama bear in me stayed to watch practice anyway.

He went to meet his team. I opened my book. The coach told the boys to pair up and kick the ball with another player. My son began kicking with your son.

I guess my son decided he wasn't up for a repeat of last weekend and whatever was coming, he wanted to face it head-on. Because, after the boys had kicked the ball a few times, I heard,

Hi, I'm Ethan.

Then some running and kicks.

Hey, I'm William.

There was more ball-chasing and kicking. I looked up to see Ethan with the ball stopped under his foot. Then he looked at your son and his very next words were,

Hey, William… I'm Jewish.

At this point in her story, I felt the air leave my chest. William was so little. He was too young to understand all the complexities of Ethan's declaration. All I could do was bite my lip and hold on to hope for her next words. My head was spinning the possible scenarios. And my prayers were immediate, *Oh Lord, please let this be okay. Whatever William did, whatever happened, please show me how to make this right.*

The mother of Ethan continued:

I looked at my son and realized what he was doing. I could see it in his little-boy eyes. He wasn't going to be caught off-guard like last weekend, so I think he decided it was better to get everything on the table. I could see him steadying himself on that ball, determined to be strong, no matter the response.

Then your son looked at my son, shrugged his shoulders and said, "Well, Jesus was a Jew."

My son cracked a little smile. Your son couldn't have cared less. And they ran off together kicking and laughing.

All I could think in that moment was, I really want to meet William's mom.

I almost fell to the ground with thankfulness. I mean, for goodness' sake, you try to teach your son right. You hope you've put some wisdom in their hearts. But in a moment like that. When they're young like that. That story could have gone a million ways. I bless God for that moment, full of innocence for William and full of healing for Ethan.

What began as a powerful moment between two little boys became an even sweeter story for us all. After one Jewish announcement and one Christian response, Ethan and William became the best of friends. His mom, Leslie, became my girlfriend. And our families had the privilege of doing life together for several years. Cookouts, boat rides on the lake, weekend soccer tournaments, games and practices, Ethan's bar mitzvah, and eventually the celebration of our wedding. We live hours away from each other now but think of them often, miss our time together, and will always be grateful God brought us together.

In the years since, our sons have made friends with boys of many faiths and many backgrounds. When the heart leads with kindness instead of judgment, then the soul of a person becomes the most important thing. Not color or faith background or country of origin or historical data. When you meet a person and first consider their soul, especially when that person is a teenage boy, there is a sweet opportunity to represent our Jesus as He claimed to be:

> For God so loved the world that he gave his only Son, that whoever believes in him shall not perish but have eternal life. For God did not send his Son into the world to condemn the world, but to save the world through him (John 3:16-17).

We're honored to welcome boys into our home who don't believe like us. The honor becomes even greater if we have the opportunity to discuss our faith, address misunderstandings or wrong impressions, or maybe even bring healing where others have given wounds.

I am not naïve about these thoughts. I do understand we live in a world full of great religious divides. Evil abounds in many hearts. And there are untold numbers of wolves dressed in sheep's clothing.

But I also believe our sons can become the kind of men who are not afraid to rebuild bridges, fight against evil, and expose deceit. They will be great men who

- reject prejudice
- delay judgment
- reason with wisdom

- show kindness to others
- see one another through the eyes of Jesus

Thankfully, for today, most of our sons will go outside to play with the worries of this world still far away. Their tiny shoulders still unburdened by what might be and the burdens they will carry. Their minds still free from weighty discussions and divisions.

So for today, while they are ours, and while we have this influence, let us fill their hearts with kindness. There will be enough differences to sort out down the road. Let us teach them to give what we have been given.

A Son Needs His Mom to

Move Heaven and Earth for All His Lasts

For where your treasure is, there will your heart be also.

Luke 12:34

I was a single mom with four kids.

William was eight or nine, I think.

However old he was, I had finally gotten that boy signed up for a soccer team in our neighborhood. The league was one of those low-stress, we-just-want-these-boys-to-have-a-good-time kind of leagues. Just my speed. Truth is, we didn't care what kind of league we were in because William was playing soccer and he was happy. So I was happy.

About two months into our low-stress and low-commitment league, a sweet soccer dad asked if I would consider letting William play club soccer. Then he tried to explain to me what club soccer is. I'm not exactly sure what he said, but what I heard was lots of practice, lots of games, travel to weekend tournaments, and monthly dues. I told that dad we were happy where we were and I couldn't see any reason to move to a different league. Besides, William was just a little boy and it was just soccer.

Then that dad said these two things: "I'm happy to stop by your house and take him back and forth to practice. And Angela, maybe you don't realize this, but William already has the kind of soccer skill that could pay for his college one day."

I signed him up.

Little did I know back then how much joy the great sport of soccer would bring to our family. All the years since have been filled with other parents who became our friends, coaches who became good influences, and the crazy fun we've enjoyed laughing and cheering together over a bunch of boys chasing a ball filled with air. (Thank you, Coach Reitnour, for that consistent reminder.)

One of William's first great coaches was Jason Barnes. The team had a travel tournament coming up and my schedule was jammed. Jason said he'd watch over William. Another family offered to let him bunk in their room. I was grateful for the help and figured William would have the best weekend ever without his mama hanging around.

On Sunday afternoon, the team was headed home and Jason called me from his car. Evidently, William hadn't been himself all weekend and everybody noticed. He wasn't sick and he wasn't hurt, but he hadn't played like they knew he could. Jason told me he and the other parents decided William had not been himself because I wasn't there. *What? Really?* I was honestly shocked. I love William and he loves me, but I couldn't imagine that my presence, or lack of it, mattered to his game.

Besides, I was such a newbie soccer mom, half the time I had no idea why the ref blew the whistle or why people were always yelling, "Offsides!" Coach Jason talked to William after the tournament. As best I can remember, he told me part of his talk went like this,

William, the way you play soccer is a gift God gave to you. When you use that gift, it glorifies Him. I know you miss having your mom here, but I want you to understand something. As followers of Jesus, we're called to do everything—soccer, math problems, making the bed, everything—unto the Lord. Your mom will not always be on the sidelines cheering, but even when she is, I want you to play soccer to honor the One who gave strong legs and a sharp mind.

By the time Jason finished our call I was one teary mom. Grateful for our godly coach. And humbled by the reminder that being a mom in the stands really matters.

A few years ago, William turned the majority of his focus and energy toward his academics, a decision we whole-heartedly affirmed. But he wisely kept soccer in his life for a million great reasons. He has the opportunity to play for a once-in-a-lifetime kind of coach, whose mission includes using soccer to build great men. His varsity teammates have become a band of brothers. And on this team, the seniors become servant leaders.

As his senior year approached, I had some personal decisions to make. My work usually takes me out of town on Friday nights, especially in the fall. In years past, I made it to a lot of games, but heartbreakingly missed too many special nights. Important things like state playoffs and the Homecoming game I planned to attend, until the school had a conflict and changed the date. I've never cried so hard, standing atop a mountain in California trying to get enough cell coverage to video chat with my kids all dressed up for the Homecoming Banquet back in North Carolina without me.

On one hand, there was no real decision for me to make. It's his last year of varsity soccer, for heaven's sake. On the other hand, fall is the busiest travel season I have, full of amazing opportunities to teach. And then, truthfully, every time I thought about cutting my three most productive months of tuition-paying income, I'd feel kinda queasy. A smarter woman would have made some financial preparations for such a big income slash. But I had decided even if it meant incurring debt, I was staying home for my son's last year. Obviously, a financial advisor, I am not.

But this one is the last one.

So, this year, I told the Athletic Director to have that Homecoming anytime he wants. Change the date. Move that thing around two or three times if he wants to. Because whenever it's happening, I'm going to be there.

To move heaven and earth not to miss his lasts has been the easiest decision I ever made.

Nowadays, William knows Who he plays for. And Scott has finally taught me what *offsides* means. But after the game, no matter the score, I'm the happiest mom on the planet.

Eventually, my son comes across the field and hugs me. I kiss him and say, "Good game, peanut." I can smell his stinky jersey. He gives me some books to carry. Our family lingers behind the bleachers, retelling the big plays, laughing with the other parents, and high-fiving their boys whom we love like our own.

Somebody decides where to go eat and we all head to our cars.

And the night air hangs thick around me with truth.

The game doesn't matter.

Whatever I'm missing out there on the road doesn't matter.

But this I know for sure: There is nothing sweeter. There is no honor or accolade more important. There is no greater joy than being his mama and sitting in the bleachers for all his lasts.

47

A Son Needs His Mom to
Count the Days

For a thousand years in your sight are but as yesterday
when it is past, or as a watch in the night.

Psalm 90:4

just took William to his first day of preschool.

Blink.

Yesterday, he began his last year of high school.

Blink. Blink.

And the whole thing went exactly like they said.

When I gave birth to my baby, they told me to take it all in because the days would go fast, and I nodded. When I wondered if he'd ever sleep through the night, they warned me not to wish away one day. I thought I understood. Today, everything in me wants to yell, *Would the whole, wide world please stop talking to me about college? Don't you know that my boy just started preschool?! And while you're at it, would you all stop rushing me along? I'm just about to figure out how to be his mom.*

But here we are. It's William's senior year.

For the record, every smart person who admonished me with a sassy, *Oh, honey, he'll be grown before you know it,* was right. They were so dang right. And this very minute, it's awful how completely right they still are. I have officially decided to never say that to anybody, ever. When you cannot change the length of one day, it kills you to be reminded, over and over, of how it's all gonna be gone before you know it. Then, when they're right, and the years are gone, you're mad at everybody who ever said it.

My first 18 years on this earth lasted an eternity. I was there. I lived them. And I can still testify to the truth of it. Growing up took forever. When the first 18 years feel like an eternity, a mom cannot anticipate what will happen on the day her baby takes his first breath. I'll tell you what happened. When my son was born, his first breath turned science on its head and blew up every space-time theory I memorized in physics.

Scholars might define *time* as the continued progression of existence and events in apparently irreversible succession. Then mathematicians would add that when you use the same interval (one year) to measure the same progression (the earth's trip around the sun), the answer will always be the same. One year is one lap around the solar system, is four seasons, is twelve months, is 365ish days. When our boys become 18, they will have circled the same sun, and celebrated on the same day, the same number of times. The time that measures their years is all the same, scientifically speaking.

Moms with seniors in high school know all that gobbledygook is a big, fat lie.

Science, schmience.

Something happens the day they are born that quantum physics cannot explain. It's a factor for which science has no measure. When a mother falls in love with her child, equations can no longer compute the length of days. The earth may circle the sun at exactly the same pace, but when days have been wrapped in a mother's love, time is never measured the same. And this is the thing no one tells you.

To love a child changes everything. Every. Single. Thing.

All the science breaks down in the light of a mother's love. Theories get rewritten. Logic is ruined. And time—well, when a mother loves a child, the time we have will never be enough.

If you're not there yet, one of those days will finally be the first day of your son's senior year. On that day, here's what I want you to do.

Make sure you walk him outside where you can take his smirky first-day-of-school picture. Stand there and smile while he runs back into the house for things he's forgotten. The years have taught you well and now it's fun to know what's coming. Watch him get all that stuff into his car, readjust his seat, and then take way too long to find just the right back-to-school music. Now wave like crazy as he backs his car down the drive and then turns it toward the most exciting year he's ever known. This is a good day, I promise. You've worked like a mad woman to keep that boy alive and get him safely here. It's a really good day.

When you're back in the house, I want you to take a few quiet minutes to count it all up. The years. The days. The adventures. The tears. Before you leave the quiet, factor this last equation. Add these things together:

All his years
+ all that you've given
+ all the places
+ all the people
+ every obstacle
+ every victory

I can tell you in advance, the sum total of your memories will not equal anything close to eighteen years. The math falls apart every time. You see, God gives moms a greater gift with an equation that usually goes like this:

His days + all your memories x the power of a mother's love = *a blink*.

If you count every one of his days until they are done and the sum total of it all is a blink, get down on your hands and knees and praise the One who entrusted that boy to your love. God has given you a beautiful gift.

It's the kind of gift that makes me wonder. When a mother's love counts the days, is that the tiniest foreshadowing of what is yet to be? Maybe when we are in the presence of God's love, trying to count eternity by years will require another kind of calculation altogether.

A hymn writer seemed to be thinking about that very thing when he wrote, "My soul will sing your praise unending, ten thousand years and then forevermore." Just maybe it was God's plan all along. Maybe, when we have known a mother's love for her child, we have tasted the great love of heaven.

So yes, I will never again say to anyone, *That baby will be grown and gone before you know it.* When I see a sweet mama holding her new baby, I think what I'm supposed to say is this:

I pray God does for you what He did for me. I hope when your boy is grown and the years have gone by, all those days feel to you like a blink. I've learned that the only way a length of years can ever equal a blink is when they have been lived in the presence of indescribable love.

Oh sister, I hope you blink.

48

A Son Needs His Mom to

Teach Him to Be Hipster (In the Best Possible Way)

There is nothing better for a person than that he should eat and drink and find enjoyment in his toil. This also, I saw, is from the hand of God, for apart from him who can eat or who can have enjoyment?

Ecclesiastes 2:24-25

I am the daughter of a produce man.

Long before it was cool, my dad and his brother owned a fruit stand on the side of the road. They had the kind of family business where the family part was assumed. If you were in the family, you were in the fruit stand business. The children weren't asked what they'd like to do one day, because it didn't really matter. When you were tall enough to see over the counter, it was time to go to work!

From age ten until I was a sophomore in college, my work was only a few days a week through the summer and a six-hour shift most Saturdays. At Christmas, the whole family would pitch in to make hundreds of fruit baskets for corporate employee gifts. By Christmas Eve, we'd be frozen and exhausted. In the summer, when produce was plentiful, we'd be hot and exhausted, but not one of us remembers those years with any resentment. As a matter of fact, when I'm with my cousins, all of our best stories are fruit stand stories. I think they'd all agree each one of us was profoundly shaped by the simple, hard work we did together.

Turns out, we were totally hipster back then, decades ahead of our time. At Thomas Fruit Stand, we were all about local, organic, retro, reclaimed, vintage, homespun, farm-to-table, homemade, and artisanal. A wood-stove kept us warm in the winter. Mama made quilts and apple butter and canned beans every summer. Everything we sold at the fruit stand came from a garden or farm or somebody's kitchen.

My children will tell you, to this day, I have a soft spot for fruit stands and farmer's markets. If there is a card table on the side of the road with a few tomatoes, a couple of cucumbers, and a handwritten *Homegrown* sign, it's over. I'll swerve across lanes of traffic, make U-turns, even drive through an occasional field to get to that person who has something honest and local to sell. The smells. The total lack of pretense. The beauty of it all. Oh my, local markets are my jam. A forever hipster at heart.

Which is why I'm so encouraged by this generation and their renewed appreciation for good, healthy foods, their support for local sellers, and the revival of handcrafted arts. In a complex world that keeps moving faster than the Internet can report, a new generation is recognizing the beauty of invested time, hard work, and craftsmanship. I love it all.

In our lifetime, Doritos might always be the king of snack. Mass production and cheap goods might always be the most cost-effective strategy. But for our boys' own good, let's teach them a little about being hipster, in the best possible way.

In our house, I can't possibly buy everything organic, so I pick and choose, buying as much food as I can from local growers, even having a little garden in our backyard most summers. Sometimes we are forced to get store-bought veggies, but I've tried to teach my children that homegrown is better, every time. I drag them to craft fairs, introducing the boys to artisans, because I want them to value the honest things people can produce with hard work. I say things like, "No store-bought cookie is worth the calories to me. I'm saving all my calories for a taste of something homemade." Years ago I was just like everybody else, driving through McDonalds for a kid's meal without a real understanding of what we were eating. But that woman has learned and I don't want my children to make the same mistakes. If they yell, "Fast food!" from the backseat, they're gonna hear, "No way," from this mama.

Now, here's the thing. All the food in our pantry is not organic. All our furniture is not handmade. I'm not as great at repurposing as I want to be. We still have too much plastic everything. Most of our furniture is the mass-produced kind that will be leaning in a few years. I didn't make our clothes or the curtains or tan hides for their shoes. We are as modern-day as they come.

But oh, how I long for them to appreciate and embrace the best of our old fruit stand values. The joy of hard work. Frugality. Kindness to everyone, especially those who are hungry. The goodness of fresh food, naturally grown, simply eaten. To appreciate all the things people do with their hands—a stunning garden, a beautiful meal, a jar of jelly, the words in a book, music, art, a hand-built house, or a freshly swept front porch.

I want my boys to become men who stop for farm stands. The kind who talk kindly to people selling peaches or kites or whatever. Men who ask questions about how things are made and appreciate that person's work, no matter their appearance or their education or how incredibly different that person might be. I want them to choose organic over processed every time they can. I want them to find value in sweeping a good floor, making a meal for their family, and building a warm fire on a snowy day. I hope they know some of the best things are slow, even as the world shouts to them, *faster, faster.*

I'm joking when I say teach your boys to be *hipster.* I'm no sociologist and really don't understand all the word even means. All I know is that some of today's hipsters esteem the same kind of things I learned at the fruit stand. If a part of being *hipster* means having an appreciation for honest values and honest foods and honest materials, then that's the part of hipster I hope takes hold in their souls.

Besides, teaching them a little hipster is way cooler than, *Son, come over here and let Mama tell you what I learned growing up at the fruit stand...*

49

A Son Needs His Mom to

Prepare Him for Greater Things

*For we are his workmanship, created in Christ
Jesus for good works, which God prepared
beforehand, that we should walk in them.*

Ephesians 2:10

Several years ago, I was introduced to the work of the Christian organization World Vision. Their ministry is dedicated to working with children, families, and communities around the world. One of the beautiful ways World Vision fights poverty is through their child sponsorship program that links caring sponsors to children in great need.

Since I first heard about the children and their great need, our family has made commitments to sponsor nine children, five in Africa and four in Bolivia. These past years of connection to our sponsor children have been a great way to teach our natural children so many tender and powerful lessons. We exchange letters, send gifts, and get regular updates about their schooling and activities, complete with pictures!

But two years ago, something life-changing happened for our family. The six of us were honored to travel with World Vision for ten days in Bolivia. The main purpose of our trip was the opportunity for me to more fully see and understand the effect World Vision is having in over 100 countries. I had previously traveled to witness their work in South Africa, but this time, our entire family was going. I was beside myself with joy. I couldn't wait to introduce my children to the sights and sounds of another country, so very different from our own.

By the time we reached our first village, there had been three flights with the final landing at one of the highest-altitude airports in the world.

We packed into a tiny van for a middle-of-the-night escapade down the mountain into La Paz. The next day we met with the national leaders at the Bolivian World Vision headquarters and then squeezed into more cars for the five-hour drive to our first stop, which felt like it had to be somewhere in the vicinity of the ends of the earth. Truly. I have never seen such a desolate, beautiful place. The altitude was so high and the distance was so far, I kept thinking to myself, *How could there possibly be people out here?* Quickly followed by, *If people live where we are going, how in the world did someone find them?*

Our next days were filled with eye-opening, heart-stopping, awe-inspiring encounters with, quite possibly, the happiest people I've ever met. Every new Bolivian sight and sound was amazing, and the landscape was unlike anything we'd ever seen. But to this day, our most precious memories are the days spent with our sponsored children and their families. Real, wonderful children who live so very far away, and yet their hearts and needs are so much the same. We sang songs and played soccer and ate more llama than I knew existed.

One morning while we were there, I woke a little early to spend time praying for our day. Somewhere in my prayers, I began thanking God for our time in Bolivia and somehow my praying started sounding like this,

Lord, thank You for bringing me to this amazing place. Thank You for eyes to see You are here and the opportunity to witness what You are doing. Teach me while I am here. Show me what to do with what I am seeing. Direct me by Your Word. I want to help and serve. Lord, use me.

I was praying my heart out that morning, and I do believe God graciously heard and received all my prayers. But before I was even finished praying, there was something like a shout into my spirit. Here's what I believe I heard from God:

Angela, thank you for those prayers. But actually, this trip is much bigger than you. I brought your family to Bolivia to teach your children. They will do greater things than you ever dreamed.

Can I just tell you how much that Holy Spirit interruption meant to me? I began to cry tears of joy, humbled, and almost sobbing. It had never occurred to me to begin preparing them for an even greater work than I will ever see. Just after college, I was absolutely sure God called me to a lifetime of ministry. That morning felt like receiving the next install-ment of His call.

To prepare my children for greater things.

Since that day in Bolivia, I have become ever more aware of my assign-ment. Now that my sons are teenagers and the years with them constantly under my roof are almost gone, I feel a sense of urgency to give them experiences and have conversations that might help prepare them for the greater things.

I talk to them more openly about peoples' struggles, both here at home and far away. When they were little that kind of talk was mostly inappro-priate and scary, but little by little, they need to know more.

I'm working hard to communicate to them a compassion for the impoverished, victims, and those caught in chains of addiction and pain. No one meant to end up in any of those places. Each one is hurting and needs help.

Jesus said, "Everyone to whom much was given, of him much will be required, and from him to whom they entrusted much, they will demand the more" (Luke 12:48). I hope to impart to them both the duty and the blessing of obeying Jesus. With a great education, for example, comes the responsibility of using that education for good and God's glory. I hope they begin to understand the duty that comes with so many of their blessings.

We are more intentional about conversations concerning world events, hoping they'll take interest, knowing more about the key leaders, their countries, and the struggles they face. Sons who don't know what's going on in their world are not prepared for greater things.

I have felt strongly about keeping most of my compassionate acts hid-den, even from my children. Not tooting my horn when there was an opportunity to help or to serve. These days, I am more intentional about including the kids in quiet acts of service and compassion where there is no fanfare and no record kept for the sake of college applications.

I am learning to expand my own interests so there is more to give to these sons who need depth. But at the same time, I want to know the great value of simple things and slower days. Into the unhurried life and unclut-tered mind, God can speak greater things.

Sometimes, I wish I'd heard God shout to me sooner, but I trust His timing was perfect for us. But maybe with this reading, you will begin preparing your son sooner than me.

Most every mom I know longs to prepare her son to become a great man.

I believe God has called us to more.

May we prepare our sons to become great men and with their lives, do even greater things than our minds can even conceive.

50

A Son Needs His Mom to

Show Him How to Do the Hardest Thing First

Whatever your hand finds to do, do it with your might.

Ecclesiastes 9:10

This may well be the most straightforward and powerful piece of advice ever spoken:

Do the hardest thing first.

Period. End of message. Nothing to dissect, ponder, or argue about. There is no philosophical worldview to embrace or deny. No hemming or hawing about it. This life-changing adage is so simple. Just wake up every day and jump on the hardest thing. Do it before your head has time to talk you out of it or your body has spent the energy required to face it.

Do the hardest thing first. Every day. With every assignment.

I'm not sure how I missed something so easy to communicate, but I cannot ever remember hearing this principle as a child, or even as a teenager. I wasted a lot of time in my early adult years trying to work up to the hard things. Checking the no-brainers off my to-do list first. Delaying the inevitable hard thing with just one more procrastinating thing.

My mental approach was something more akin to stretching before exercising. I guess I was afraid to pull a brain muscle, so instead of diving into the tough thing, I'd end up doing mental and emotional circles around it. My circles came complete with hand-wringing, worrying, lots of list-making, and the ever-spiritual practice of endless prayer about the hard thing. I grieve all the time I have wasted in my life just doing circles. And besides the lost time, the circles unknowingly began to cultivate a lifestyle of stress and anxiety. A lifestyle that had to be unlearned as an adult.

It's a million times harder to retrain your adult-self to stop the crazy-maker circles and face the hardest thing first, so we must teach our sons while they are young. And, as with most everything in this book, we best teach what we have fought to learn for ourselves.

As an adult, still being retrained, here are some of the things I have learned about doing the hardest thing first.

Sometimes the hardest thing that day felt like it might involve conflict. Delaying the hard thing taught me to be conflict-avoidant instead of teaching me to be a gracious conflict-resolver.

Most of the things my head labeled as hard didn't turn out to be very hard at all. I can be an exaggerator especially for the purpose of procrastination. Most of the things other people told me were going to be hard didn't turn out to be very hard either. Other people can exaggerate too.

Doing the hardest thing first cultivates strength of character. Doing circles around the hardest thing cultivates weakness and greater insecurity.

I have many times delayed facing the hardest things because of my fears and insecurities. Some of my fears are reasonable ones based on my life experiences. Learning to do the hardest thing first has taught me the difference between real fear and fabricated fear. Fabricated fear is the kind of "life drama" I don't want any part of.

Facing the hardest thing first requires an optimistic attitude. The pessimist keeps doing circles.

Even when something turned out to be the hardest thing I'd ever done, to have it behind me instead of still in front of me was both a great and peace-giving accomplishment.

I speak from years of experience when I say most of us are easily intimidated by big, hard things. We label the hard thing *impossible* and decide it just can't be done. So we don't even try, and the hard thing wins, and life is remembered by what could have been.

May it never be for our sons! I don't want my sons to live in the bogged-down rut of procrastination. I don't want them to live afraid of hard things or too insecure to attempt the things this world calls "hard." As their mom,

I know they were made for so much more than to grow up and live stuck. Life is too precious and their purpose too great to be wasted.

Training our sons to do the hardest thing involves two necessary skills:

Overcomer thinking.

Get-up-and-get-going doing.

Overcomer thinkers know there are very few things in life that are completely and totally impossible. Most hard things have a solution. I may not have the answer, but I can ask for help until I find someone who does. Overcomer thinkers are not afraid of what they don't know. They keep their hearts open to learning and growing as they overcome new, hard things.

Get-up-and-get-going doers don't delay when there is something hard to be done. They have to mow the grass over the weekend, so they get it done first thing on Saturday. They have an English paper to write, so with the two hours they have free, they head to the library to begin. Not doing the hard thing first is procrastination. And procrastination quickly becomes a habit when our thinking is filled with fears and insecurity.

When you teach your son to do the hardest things first, you build a strong work ethic into his character. You teach him to become a creative thinker. A solution finder. A problem solver.

You affirm to him that his mind is capable. His body is able. He can do more than he even realizes. You ground him in the beautiful truth of Scripture: Whatever your hand finds to do, do it with all of your heart. You set him up to live with purpose, unhindered by groundless fears and insecurities.

When you show your son how to do the hardest things first, the temptation of trivial things will lose their power to distract. And greater things he may have missed will become his purpose and his joy.

So I pray for you and me that we will model and teach these truths to our sons.

Hard things are great things waiting to happen.

Hard things are victories waiting to be celebrated.

Hard things are legacies waiting to be written.

51

A Son Needs His Mom to

Show Him It's Okay When Good Work Makes You Tired

Whatever you do, work heartily, as for the Lord and not for men.

Colossians 3:23

As far as I can tell, the two boys God chose for me are regular, run-of-the-mill kind of boys. They have always been the kind who can spend hours kicking a soccer ball or riding a skateboard, completely undeterred by pouring rain, hunger pains, or a little blood. Just like most boys, when they are doing something they love they are all in. Time stands still. The world falls away. They are focused. Determined. Tireless.

Nobody works harder at having fun than boys.

But when they were little, the craziest thing would happen. If I mentioned unloading the dishwasher or running upstairs to get dirty laundry, those energetic, oblivious-to-pain little boys would nearly collapse. Their legs would buckle underneath the weight of their exhaustion. Headaches appeared. Homework was remembered. You'd think I'd asked them to fetch laundry from Mount Everest or empty a canyon of dishes. They'd look at me like, *What kind of mother would ask such difficult things of regular, run-of-the-mill boys?* Besides, they were hungry. And their legs could barely move.

Oh, the great burden of work when you could be playing your heart out instead.

When a healthy body is able to play with boundless energy but falls down in the presence of work, there is a problem moms have to address.

The Bible says each one of us is born with a sin nature. It's the part of us that wants to choose the wrong thing even when we know the right thing to do. Because of our nature, pleasure can many times trump responsibility, especially when dirty dishes are involved. And because it's more fun to choose play, little boys might be inclined to fall down at the mention of work. Great men, though, have learned to step up when work is required. Our sons are great men in training.

But here's where teaching boys to choose work gets hard. Sometimes it's just easier to do something myself than direct and redirect a whiny toddler (or teenager) to choose work. The truth is, it's always going to be easier to rinse a cereal bowl in peace than call my son downstairs to ask him to rinse his bowl and put it in the dishwasher. Shoot, I can rinse and load twenty bowls in the time it takes me to yell from the bottom of the stairs three times, finally go up to knock on his door, talk to a groggy person taking a nap, and then stand in his room until two feet are on the floor slugging toward the kitchen.

For the love. I'd rather do it myself. Always.

But when I do it myself, I have forsaken my job as his mom. In this little family, I am a Vice President of Domestic Training. Thankfully the Lord runs this place, but I've still got a job to do, which is why I must keep my assignment in mind.

Our goal is to raise sons who become mature, responsible men of God.

When I remember my assignment, then I decide not to do that thing he should have done. And I choose to push through any forgetfulness or excuses or blank stares because the world needs more great men who don't live with their mamas anymore.

From their earliest days we should teach our sons that *work* is not a four-letter word to be avoided at any cost. They need to understand that purposeful work is good. To provide for a family and a home is good, purposeful work. Some days good work means executing an exciting business plan. Other days, it means raking leaves in the backyard.

We mentor them as we do good work in front of them. We instruct them as we speak and dream of good work to be done. We inspire them as we, many days, work until we're tired and then praise God for the blessing of doing work that matters.

Mature, responsible men have learned to stand up when there is work to be done. Even if that work might make them tired. Even if they have to do it alone. Even if it takes longer than planned. Even when there are obstacles. And even if no one applauds, says thank you, or puts the name of their good work up in lights.

Mature men are able to delay pleasure until the work has been done.

Mature men will choose necessary, hard work, even if it makes them tired.

Mature men are independent and able to choose work without prodding, prompting, or sulking.

And after good work, we rest and play and worship the One who makes us able.

52

A Son Needs His Mom to

Give His Nintendo 64 to the Homeless Shelter

Whoever brings blessing will be enriched, and
one who waters will himself be watered.

Proverbs 11:25

Before I begin, I'd just like to say one thing. When this little event happened, I truly had no idea.

About 12 years ago, I was a single mom with four young children. I was also our only financial provider. Actually, Jesus was our Provider and most of my problems came on the days I was a forgetter. I'm embarrassed to tell you how often I'd be right in the middle of a full-blown panic attack, wondering how in the world that month's bills would be paid, before I'd remember whose I am. How much He loves me. And all those promises He has made to us.

> Therefore I tell you, do not be anxious about your life, what you will eat or what you will drink, nor about your body, what you will put on...Look at the birds of the air: they neither sow nor reap nor gather into barns, and yet your heavenly Father feeds them. Are you not of more value than they?...But if God so clothes the grass of the field...will he not much more clothe you, O you of little faith? (Matthew 6:25-30).

Thankfully, God is always faithful and especially gracious to forgetful mamas like me.

In those years, our family of five lived as frugally as we could. I wanted to honor God's provision by taking care of our things and teaching the children to take care of their toys. Whatever we had really needed to last, and I wanted them to understand all we had were gifts from the hand of God, to be cared for instead of neglected.

At that time, according to their calculation, my two boys were the very last people on the planet who did not have the newest video game system called PlayStation. We only had the old Nintendo 64 system that seemed to work just fine for me. But Christmas was coming, so I saved a little money each month until I could finally get the fancy new game box that would surprise those two on Christmas morning.

Come Christmas day, that sparkling new PlayStation did just what I'd hoped it would do. It sent two little boys to the moon with joy and gratitude. They were SO HAPPY to have their very own coolest toy ever built. The Nintendo 64 was unplugged from the TV and quickly replaced by the shiny new PlayStation. From that day forward, it was all about the Play-Station at my house. Or so I thought.

I'm not sure how much time lapsed between that joyous Christmas morning and what happened next. Maybe it was a month. Maybe three. I'm not really sure. But, one day it occurred to me that there were probably little boys at the homeless shelter who didn't have video games to play and they'd probably be tickled to death with an old Nintendo 64. So I went straight home and loaded that thing up—the game box, cords, plugs, and all the games I could find. Donkey Kong, Super Mario, Madden NFL, and Smash Brothers. Then I toted every Nintendo thing we had down to the homeless shelter. The administrator was happy to receive all our stuff and that made me happy.

Remember, I had no idea.

Sometime after I gave that thing away, maybe a few more months, the boys came looking for me. "Mom, have you seen our Nintendo 64?"

"I have."

"We can't find it. Where did you put it?"

"Well, after you guys got the PlayStation, I thought the boys at the homeless shelter might like your Nintendo, so I loaded it up and gave it to them."

Grayson and William were appalled. "You *what*?" they asked.

"I gave it to little boys who don't have any games. Actually, they don't even have a house, so I thought some video games would be fun for them."

Unmoved by the plight of the homeless and my rationale, they pleaded, "Why did you give away our Nintendo?"

"Because you guys got a brand new PlayStation for Christmas. The Nintendo was just sitting there. I thought some other little boys might enjoy it."

"MOM, that was ours. We were going to play it again. The Nintendo was special. It was a keepsake."

"I'm sorry, guys. I didn't think you'd miss it because you were so crazy about the PlayStation. It's gone and I can't get it back. Besides, some other boys are happy."

Unmoved by my generosity or the thought of other boys being happy, they made sure I understood how they felt, "Mom, this is awful. You didn't even ask. You just gave away all our great games. We wanted to keep those games."

Needless to say, I had no idea how those two felt about their Nintendo 64 video games. *Out with the old, in with the new*, was my mindset. Really, I had no idea.

At least once a year since the Nintendo fiasco, both of my boys have reminded me of the time I gave away their precious Nintendo 64. Today, the boys are 20 and 18, and when I asked them about it, they still sounded like they were remembering a death. *When I gave. Their Nintendo. Away.*

Here's the honest truth. I'd give that Nintendo away again in a flat minute.

But, if I could do the whole thing over, I'd give it away differently next time.

If I could go back, I'd tell the boys we didn't need the Nintendo anymore and we were going to take it to some boys who don't have any video games. I'd load the boys up with the games and drive them to the homeless shelter. I'd call the administrator in advance and ask for a time that my boys could come and set up their Nintendo in the rec area. I'd get permission for my boys to teach other boys how to play Mario and Donkey Kong. Then I'd walk them in and let them receive the joy of giving what they no longer needed. I wouldn't care if they were pouty in the car.

I wouldn't listen if they said they wanted to keep their dust-catching Nintendo as a keepsake.

But, if I could do it over, I would include them in the joy.

Most of the time giving matters more than keeping. What the heck are keepsakes but a bunch of junk in my attic? I'd much rather those things bring laughter and smiles to children today than be auctioned off at flea markets in 20 years.

Sons need their moms to teach them how to give their precious things to others. I didn't do the greatest job with this lesson, but oh, how I hope you can do better than me!

May our boys come to understand the beauty of enjoying something for a while and then multiplying their joy by giving it away.

53

A Son Needs His Mom to

Teach Him to Give a Little More Than Required

And as you wish that others would do to you, do so to them.

Luke 6:31

I am so very honored that you spent hard-earned money to buy this book of 52 things. When you plopped down those dollars or clicked a "Buy Now" button, I imagine you expected 52 good and valuable things. I hope you feel like these 52 were worth your time and money. I hope you have been encouraged.

But if it's okay with you, I'd like to offer you one more thing. I realize you never gave one thought to the possibility that we straight-up lied to you on the cover. My publisher only asked me for 52. I signed a writing contract for 52, and because I checked, there are no clauses in that fancy publishing contract that might prevent me from giving more to you than I promised.

Please accept this last thing as my gift. I wanted you to get more from this little book than you bargained for. A little something extra. A surprise where none was expected. I wanted you to have a little more without any fanfare. And without a slick huckster shouting, "Buy 52 and get one free!"

This extra thing is both a message and the point of the message.

Sons need their moms to teach them to give a little more than required. Without any fanfare. Without resentment. And without the expectation of ever being repaid. Our guys need to learn there is joy in giving or doing something where nothing was expected.

Many days, my husband wears a wristband that reads, "Exceed Expectations." Last year, he had hundreds of those wristbands printed to give to his coworkers. He's hoping if you wear it on your wrist, you begin to remember. When someone chooses to buy or service a truck with his company, Scott wants folks to be more than satisfied. He wants them to get more than they expected.

"A little extra" is a great business strategy, and if I had a business, I'd do the same thing! Shoot, I'd probably have little reminders dinging on the computers and signs flashing overhead to remind the people in my company to consider how they might do a little more than the customer requires.

"Exceed Expectations" is also a brilliant strategy for the savvy student. Many times I'll ask my kids, "What does your teacher want from you on this assignment?" Then after I hear the whole blah, blah, blah about how much they have to do for this one thing, I'll say something like, "Okay, for the A, do all of that well, and just a little more." Fainting spells (and things that look like fainting) ensue.

But doing more than expected is just plain smart. Whether you are a businessman or a student, it's a brilliant plan that produces great rewards.

As awesome as good grades and repeat customers are, the pursuit of either one, or both, is not the intent of my final piece of advice for you. Here's the main thing about this message. I want my boys to want to do a little more even when there is no direct benefit or profit to them. Make that *especially* when there is nothing in it for them.

That sort of giving is in keeping with the spirit of Jesus's words: "If anyone wants to sue you and take your shirt, hand over your coat as well. If anyone forces you to go one mile, go with them two miles" (Matthew 5:40-41).

A follower of Jesus lives with service in view, looking for ways to do more for the people he encounters. Around my house we call it "being a blessing." But no matter how you frame it, to give more than was necessary is pure kindness. Paul told the Galatians that kindness was a "fruit of the spirit." That means kindness is one of the traits that grows in men who have a relationship with Jesus Christ.

Teaching our sons to give a little more than required can begin in the simplest ways...

Asking your toddler, "If we cut a flower from our yard as a surprise for Grandma, show me which flower you think she'll love the most."

Having a conversation with your growing boy. "When you're at recess, are there ever any boys who don't have someone to play with?"

"Yeah, there's usually this kid standing by himself. Nobody really talks to him. He's kinda mean."

"Sometimes people are mean when they're afraid of getting hurt or tired of being picked on."

Silence from the boy who is processing what you just said.

"Why don't you give this a shot. Tomorrow on the playground, run over and ask him to play with you and your friends. Give him an easy place on the team. If he says no, ask him again the next day. And the next. He might reject you every time, but at least you'll know you tried to bless him. And he'll never forget that you kept noticing him."

"But Mom, he's really mean."

"I believe you. Will you ask him anyway? I can't wait to hear what happens."

A reminder today as my high school senior ran out the door: "Why don't you take an extra juice box* for your buddy? I bet he'd like that you thought of him."

"Good call, Mom."

Teaching our sons to do a little more than required is a kindness that will fill them with joy.

Will someone take advantage of their kindness one day? Yep.

Will it hurt if their kindness is rejected? Always does.

Will their kindness be misunderstood? Count on it.

This world calls a man great for many reasons. Academic accomplishment. Business success. Military victory. Political gain. Athletic ability. Spiritual wisdom. Men who have pursued excellence are called great, as well they should be.

But when a great man is also kind?

Oh, my. May it be for my sons and for yours.

By the grace of Jesus and by the power of the Holy Spirit, may our sons become great men who are kind.

---

* Yup, he's 18. Still drinking from a juice box.

Angela Thomas is a sought-after speaker, teacher, and bestselling author of *Do You Think I'm Beautiful?*, *My Single Mom Life*, *Prayers for My Baby Boy*, and *Prayers for My Baby Girl*. She inspires thousands at national conferences, workshops, and through video studies that she filmed and wrote, including *Stronger: Finding Hope in Fragile Places*. Visit her at www.angelathomas.com.

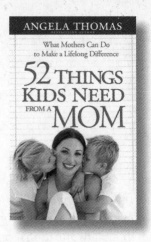

52 Things Kids Need from a Mom
What Mothers Can Do to Make a Lifelong Difference

Bestselling author and mother of four children Angela Thomas brings her trademark storytelling and biblical teaching to this book of encouragement for moms who, in the daily whir of busyness, long to connect with their kids in new ways.

With compassion and creativity, Angela presents 52 inspirations to help moms experience intentional mothering, intentional living, and intentional joy as they:

- talk to their child as though he is fascinating
- learn to play one video game
- plan activities that set a child up for success
- be the groovy mom once in a while
- make memories and savor them

Moms at all phases of parenting can adopt one idea a week or try several at once. This is a fun, guilt-free resource to help every mom lead with God's love and delight in the small moments that make up an abundant life.

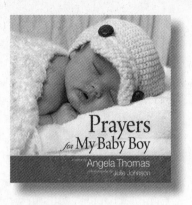

Prayers for My Baby Boy

Bestselling author Angela Thomas is an adoring mom whose prayers, presented as letters to God, celebrate a mom's delight in everyday moments with a newborn boy. Each expression of hope, gratitude, and purpose is beautifully bundled with Julie Johnson's heartwarming photos of sweet babies that are sure to spark smiles for everyone who has loved a little boy.

From the very first page, readers are reminded of the many joys and privileges of raising a child and will be led to times of prayer and thanksgiving. This tender tribute to the wonder of new life and the divine gift of motherhood will be a keepsake for all moms, grandmas, and anyone who treasures little ones.

To learn more about books by Angela Thomas or
to read sample chapters, visit our website:

www.harvesthousepublishers.com

HARVEST HOUSE PUBLISHERS
EUGENE, OREGON